W9-BXC-021

Myron Rolle is an amazing role model who is in the process of becoming a neurosurgeon after having achieved the goal of becoming a Rhodes Scholar and NFL player. His no-excuses mentality combined with a philosophy that always moves one forward is something to be emulated by all.

BENJAMIN S. CARSON SR., MD, founder and chairman, American Cornerstone Institute; emeritus professor of neurosurgery, Johns Hopkins Medicine; 17th Secretary of the United States Department of Housing and Urban Development

Myron's journey from a defensive back in the NFL to a neurosurgery suite as a cranial surgeon is an incredible example of excellence in execution and 120. Small steps cover big distances, and regular 2% improvements can mean the difference between success and failure, average and exceptional, winning and losing. *The 2% Way* will change the reader's life—I know this because it changed mine.

ERIC THOMAS, PhD, author, speaker, educator, and pastor

Dr. Myron Rolle's diverse life experience will connect with so many communities. His empathy and genius are evident in his voice and storytelling, which weave together his experiences of the most elite and world-renowned organizations. Dr. Rolle's relentless spirit is a product of Love and overcoming seemingly insurmountable adversity, and his methodology and philosophy are directly linked to the joy and success he has. His story is groundbreaking.

TROY POLAMALU, Hall of Fame strong safety for the Pittsburgh Steelers

By beautifully interweaving on- and off-field anecdotes with his 2% Way philosophy, Myron has designed a powerful playbook for tackling our greatest challenges, achieving our most daunting goals, and realizing our true potential.

BONNIE BERNSTEIN, veteran sports journalist and CEO of Walk Swiftly Productions

Dr. Myron Rolle's achievements by any standard are stellar. But I am even more proud of the commitments that inspired him to such high attainment. These include a determined, rock-solid grounding in and connection to his cultural heritage, a strong and clear life-vision pursued without fear or compromise, and a subscribed obligation to give back no matter how far his life may take him. What we are seeing is a life richly infused, and for him I believe the best is yet to come.

GLENYS HANNA MARTIN, minister of education, technical, and vocational training, government of the Bahamas

The 2% WAY

The 2% WAY

How a Philosophy of
SMALL IMPROVEMENTS
Took Me to Oxford, the NFL,
and Neurosurgery

Myron L. Rolle, MD, MSc

ZONDERVAN BOOKS

ZONDERVAN BOOKS

The 2% Way
Copyright © 2022 by Myron L. Rolle

Requests for information should be addressed to:
Zondervan, *3900 Sparks Dr. SE, Grand Rapids, Michigan 49546*

Zondervan titles may be purchased in bulk for educational, business, fundraising, or sales promotional use. For information, please email SpecialMarkets@Zondervan.com.

ISBN 978-0-310-36374-3 (audio)

Library of Congress Cataloging-in-Publication Data

Names: Rolle, Myron L., 1986– author.
Title: The 2% way: how a philosophy of small improvements took me to Oxford, the NFL, and neurosurgery / Myron L. Rolle.
Other titles: Two-percent way
Description: Grand Rapids: Zondervan, 2022. | Includes bibliographical references. | Summary: "Dr. Myron Rolle—neurosurgery resident, Rhodes Scholar, former NFL player—shares how the strong work ethic, faith, and family values instilled in him by his immigrant parents and older brothers combined with a simple-yet-transformative life philosophy to enable him to overcome adversity, defy expectations, and build a life of meaning and purpose"—Provided by publisher.
Identifiers: LCCN 2021050915 (print) | LCCN 2021050916 (ebook) | ISBN 9780310363651 (hardcover) | ISBN 9780310363668 (ebook)
Subjects: LCSH: Rolle, Myron L., 1986– | Conduct of life. | Success—Religious aspects—Christianity. | Ex-football players—United States—Biography. | Neurosurgeons—United States—Biography.
Classification: LCC BJ1547.5.R65 A3 2022 (print) | LCC BJ1547.5.R65 (ebook) | DDC 170/.44—dc23/eng/20220207
LC record available at https://lccn.loc.gov/2021050915
LC ebook record available at https://lccn.loc.gov/2021050916

Cover design: Micah Kandros
Cover photo: Enoch Kavindele Jr.
Interior design: Sara Colley

Printed in Canada

22 23 24 25 26 27 28 29 30 /FRI/ 14 13 12 11 10 9 8 7 6 5 4 3 2 1

I dedicate this book to my parents and my brothers. To Daddy, for the long car rides to boarding school where we shared the best father-son moments. To Mummy, for hugging me after all my games and telling me that I played the best game you've ever seen—even if it wasn't true. To Marchant, for teaching me how to read with Hooked on Phonics so I could stand out in my primary school classes. To Marvis, for answering my 2:00 a.m. calls to you despite the random and often esoteric topics I had on my mind. To Mordecai, for giving me your Holy Spirit High School football jersey so I could feel as unstoppable on the field as you were. To McKinley, for always reminding me that we're Rolles and should be remembered for something good that we do in this life.

We are what we repeatedly do.
Excellence, then, is not an act, but a habit.

—Will Durant

CONTENTS

ACKNOWLEDGMENTS

I want to acknowledge my wife, Latoya, for believing in me to write this book. I called you on my walk home from a twenty-four-hour shift at the hospital. You told me that I had a story to tell. A story that could change lives. I sat down in the lobby of my downtown Boston high-rise apartment and listened to you encourage me, inspire me, and motivate me to make a difference in the world through my words. I'm grateful for that conversation because it has led to this moment. Thank you, Latoya. I'm blessed to have you in my life.

PRESSURE POINTS

A newborn baby's head has a circumference of about fourteen inches. That's not much space for a neurosurgeon to operate in, especially when the procedure calls for drilling holes the size of quarters into the skull. The margin for error, already slim in brain surgery, is reduced to an almost invisible line dividing life and death.

Today's patient presented an even more challenging problem. He was delivered twelve weeks premature and now weighed only five pounds. Excess cerebrospinal fluid was trapped deep within his brain, dangerously building up pressure in a condition known as hydrocephalus. This condition is often seen in premature babies who haven't had time for their brains and blood vessels to grow fully. In developing countries, it usually stems from an infection that has passed from mother to child. In either case, the objective is to bring down the swelling, and for that, I'd need to place a ventriculoperitoneal shunt in his brain matter. The device would drain the fluid and divert it through a tube I would run behind the ear, over the clavicle, and into the stomach.

If all went well, my tiny patient would be safely in the recovery room in ninety minutes.

I'd spoken to the parents earlier in the day in the fluorescent hallway of Massachusetts General Hospital. They were a working-class couple from Somerset. The mother was calm. She'd spent the morning watching YouTube videos of the surgery and familiarizing herself with every stage of the procedure. The father was in worse shape. When he said he trusted me with his newborn's life, his handshake trembled and I could see a glint of fear in his eyes.

I have a surgeon's hands—my grip was steady. The couple didn't know that this particular surgery was the most challenging procedure for me as a neurosurgical resident.

"How's his breathing?" I asked one of the two anesthesiologists in the OR. She confirmed a healthy respiratory rate. The scrub tech and the circulating nurses checked the instruments, then rechecked them, then twice more. When you're operating on an adult, you check everything twice; with a premature newborn, you do it five times.

I took the scalpel from a sterilized metal tray and pushed it into the scalp behind the right ear. A flash of blood appeared, then the bone of the skull. I switched my scalpel for a precision drill and, using just the right amount of pressure, opened up a "burr hole." This is one of the oldest medical procedures in human history—thousands of skulls dating back to the Stone Age bear the markings of trepanation.

Next, I incised a thin layer of the dura mater, a membrane that protects the central nervous system, and saw the pink of the brain. Pink is a good sign. It shows that the organ is alive and flushed with healthy blood. If it looks like dark red currant jelly, the patient is in trouble.

I had a clear pathway to insert the catheter into the fluid-filled area in the right frontal lobe. As neurologists say, this lobe isn't as vital or "eloquent" as the left, so I slid the tube in without fear of damaging any motor or language functions.

So far, so smooth. This part of the procedure never concerned me. Since I began my residency at Harvard and Mass General in Boston three years before, I'd always seen myself as a strong cranial surgeon. My confidence is unflappable when I'm poking around in someone's head.

But when I practiced placing ventriculoperitoneal shunts (the stomach feed) with attending physicians, I had issues accessing the peritoneal cavity and moving through the layers of the abdomen. I was slow. I wasn't in the right spot. I had trouble differentiating between the fatty tissues of the belly and the much thinner ones I was supposed to cut through. When I had to make definitive moves, I faltered. I was underperforming.

That didn't sit well with me. From the day I began my residency, everyone at the hospital talked about the "NFL guy" who wanted to be a doctor. Whenever I fumbled with a pair of forceps, people noticed—or at least I did. My daddy had instilled in me a sense of perfectionism—something he viewed as necessary for a young Black boy in America. "Be so good they can't deny you," he taught me.

Perhaps my new colleagues imagined I had spent my sporting life headbutting linebackers and chugging Coors Light. They hadn't seen me run thirty-two straight 110-yard wind sprints in the Florida summer. They couldn't fathom the pressure of eighty thousand fans watching every step of your coverage. They didn't know football primed you for neurosurgery. Both require a kind of diligence that borders on fanaticism.

If a defensive back aligns himself in the right way opposite a receiver to shave off his inside routes, the back cuts off five potential plays from the receiver's route tree (the 1, 3, 5, 7, 9 for any football geeks out there). In the same vein, if I align a patient's treatment correctly, I can reduce the number of complications before we even begin. One false move is enough to bring on the cheers of the opponent's fans as a defenseman gets burned for a touchdown—or for me to hear the long, heartbreaking beep of a flatline.

I knew I had to master the ventriculoperitoneal shunt, so I adopted an approach I learned in college that has guided me through every achievement in my adult life. At Florida State, my defensive coordinator, Mickey Andrews, demanded tangible progress from his players at each practice, even if it was only a two percent improvement. "I require some small gain every day, boys!" he would yell as the safeties ran interception drills. "Someone at Alabama or Clemson is working just as hard as you. I need you to be two percent better than them in some way."

When the last whistle blew, the defense would shed their pads and congregate around a large whiteboard in the locker room. Andrews would write concepts like *technique*, *stamina*, and *toughness* on the board and ask each player if they had improved 2 percent in each metric. The team would vote on whether they felt the response was accurate. Everyone was honest in the pursuit of improvement. This goal of improving 2 percent gave me an objective every single day in practice.

Early in my college career, for example, Coach told me I needed to track the deep balls against opposing receivers. In high school, I had no problem defending pass plays because of my size and speed. But at the elite college level, I played against athletes who were as physically gifted as I was. I needed to outwork them. Every day after practice, I'd have the second-string quarterback, EJ Manuel, throw me deep passes while I turned around and sprinted, trying to knock the balls down or intercept them. I worked on timing. I worked on flight paths. I worked on turning my hips and rotating toward the ball. I waited until the last second to leap for the ball to get the maximum jump against my imaginary opponent. Within a couple of weeks, I had turned this deficiency into one of my core skill sets.

Coach Andrews learned this concept of measured improvement from Alabama legend Paul "Bear" Bryant, who called it the 2% Way. The idea has stuck with me. It's been the foundation of my success in life, from Oxford to the NFL to neurosurgery. The system works because it's a practical way to change your life for the better. You don't have to improve yourself overnight. If you improve yourself 2 percent at a time, you'll make strides without feeling overwhelmed.

You will improve yourself as a leader, a thinker, a speaker, a friend, a spouse, a parent, a Christian, or an adherent of any other belief. You can apply the 2% Way to every aspect of your life.

Armed with this philosophy, I set out to master the ventriculoperitoneal shunt procedure. I checked out all the neurosurgery training videos at the library at Mass General. I set up a film room in my apartment and studied dozens of shunt cases. By pairing visuals with the text, I was able to verbalize each step of the surgery. "Equipment: ventricular catheter, peritoneal catheter, specimen tubes for CSF, and valve," I would repeat while pacing, wearing a hole in the carpet. I wondered what my neighbors thought. "Technique: incision in the abdomen to access the peritoneal cavity. Can be done in the upper quadrant or the midline. Pass the peritoneal distal catheter between both incisions using a shunt passer."

When I needed to rehearse the procedure with someone, I called my fiancée, now my wife, and explained each step to her. If I could explain the complex surgical maneuvers to a layperson, I knew I had mastered them.

My final method of preparation was to reach out to a seasoned expert, a coach of sorts. I called Dr. Ben Warf at Boston Children's Hospital. He had spent twenty years in Uganda doing this procedure thousands of times. He was the Bear Bryant of shunts. "This surgery is important to perfect if you want to do fieldwork," he told me. "You'll do it all the time. You have to master the belly." I planned to help underserved communities in Africa, so this skill was vital. He generously spent about thirty minutes on the phone with me, going over the finer points of the technique.

Now, after all that preparation, I found myself standing over this five-pound baby in the operating room—time to make the incision. I cut into the abdomen with my scalpel and easily passed through the tissue. The blood cauterized nicely. The surgical team was calling out vital signs along with some healthy chatter. Small talk is always a good sign. The OR is deadly silent when a surgery goes off the rails.

After another shallow cut at the base of the skull, it was time for the second catheter. I sent the tube down, passing it under the skin through a series of incisions. It held in place, stopping at its intended resting place in the stomach.

I realized I had been holding my breath. I exhaled and connected the two catheters with a valve. A clear liquid rushed into the tubes. It was a beautiful sight to behold. "How's he breathing?" I asked the anesthesiologist one last time.

"Breathing just fine. Sleeping like a baby."

When the wound was closed, I scrubbed out and walked to the waiting room to update the parents. I saw the boy's father pacing around the waiting room, chewing on the collar of his coat. The mother saw me first and approached with a face that begged, "Please, please, please don't break my heart."

And I didn't.

• • •

There are thirty-two teams in the National Football League. Every year thousands of college athletes play their hearts out trying to draw the attention of the NFL. They dream to be good enough to be drafted by one of these teams.

When I came out of high school, ESPN ranked me the number one recruit in the country. When I was a junior at Florida State University, NFL draft analysts predicted that I would be selected in the first round of the following year's draft. But I had other plans. I wanted to be a member of a different elite group.

There are thirty-two Rhodes Scholarships awarded each year to students around the world. In the fall of 2008, I was awarded one of those scholarships, the first of its kind for an FSU football player. With enough credits to graduate early, I decided to accept the scholarship to Oxford for the coming year and forgo my final year of college football.

That decision would alter the course of my life forever. I had defied expectations, as I have a habit of doing, and with that came consequences. The star athlete who followed the rules suddenly became a man who went his own way. I accepted those consequences, along with all the new challenges they brought.

It's not enough to be good on paper if you don't have intangibles like grit, determination, pride, and ownership. Those intangible qualities will get you that tangible résumé of accomplishments. I was taught these values at an early age by my parents and my brothers. We are immigrants from the Bahamas who moved to the suburbs of New Jersey. Daddy taught us about the benefits of hard work and the dangers of self-pity. Mummy taught us about respect and kindness and love. My four older brothers taught me about loyalty and staying in the fight.

In this book you'll read about my journey, from a kid growing up the son of immigrants to playing prep football in New Jersey to becoming an All-American player and defensive rookie of the year at FSU to receiving a Rhodes Scholarship and trading my senior year of football for a year of study abroad at Oxford. After struggling in the NFL for a few seasons and feeling I had been viewed as an outcast for prioritizing my education over my football career, I went back to FSU for medical school. My next chapter—one I am still writing—was a neurosurgery residency with Harvard at Massachusetts General. My plan is to complete the last three years of my residency focusing on global pediatric neurosurgery. I will travel to Africa and the Caribbean, including my home country of the Bahamas, to perform neurosurgery on kids in need.

I hope my story will show you that your path in life will likely have bumps and setbacks, but with the right approach, the impossible can become possible. Little improvements over time can lead to extraordinarily positive changes. I hope it will help you step into your identity. I hope while reading you ask yourself if you are shaping who you are, or if you are letting others shape your identity for you. Audre Lorde once wrote, "Nothing I accept about myself can be used against me to diminish me."[1]

In high school, I attended three predominantly white private schools where I had to contend with the majority students but also prove myself among the small minority of other Black kids. When I went to Florida State, I faced the exact opposite problem, being thrown onto a team that felt I was "soft" because they thought I'd had it easy. In England, my love of such a brutal sport baffled my instructors. They dismissed me as a lucky anomaly to their distinguished program. After I was drafted by the Tennessee Titans, these same instructors had the guts to ask me for comp tickets to a game.

I believe in the totality of a person. Today I'm a medical doctor in a neurosurgical residency. Yet that doesn't define me. Neither does my football career or my Rhodes Scholarship. I am the sum of all my parts. The same is true for you, which means that in every part of life, you should try to continually improve yourself.

The book is for those who need inspiration amid adversity—and we face a *lot* of adversity these days. It's for the recent high school or college grad who needs to know that overcoming obstacles and improving oneself is part of the path of resilience and success. It's for the young men and women who are in the professional world but still searching for an adult identity. It's for people of color who will no doubt find the stories about discrimination in this book all too familiar but might want to adopt the pragmatic and optimistic approach I use when dealing with hate.

And finally this book is for anyone who feels that they need to improve but doesn't know where to start. My message is one of encouragement and motivation. This book will show you a better way through life: the 2% Way.

Chapter 1

YOUR LIFE IS NOT YOUR OWN

The 2% Way is a system that will allow you to steadily improve yourself. But this philosophy has a deeper component. I'm motivated to spend countless hours chipping away at my goals because I'm yoked to a sense of purpose, a spiritual foundation. If you want to fulfill your potential and find your place in the world, you must first understand what you want to achieve and why you want to achieve it. That requires examining your foundations. You are the sum of your parts, even the ones buried in the past.

When I was growing up, my parents often told me, "Myron, your life is not your own." Daddy repeated this phrase to my brothers and me over the dinner table. Mummy said it when the family drove home from church. In these words, I heard the soul-deep responsibility that many immigrant children feel toward their parents. They had sacrificed the familiarity of home to make sure my brothers and I had every opportunity. The debt I felt toward that sacrifice expressed itself in the form of my need to excel in everything I did. From a young age, I understood that the reason to better myself was to serve others, just as my parents had done.

Daddy was born in 1950 in the Bahamas's capital city of Nassau on the island of New Providence. His father, my granddaddy, was a construction worker who had migrated from the nearby island of Exuma. Exuma is one of the Family Islands—seven hundred islands and cays that circle New Providence. It is one of the twenty or so of the Family Islands that is inhabited, and Bahamians tell visitors that astronauts have identified the sparkling waters of Exuma from space. I've never had an astronaut verify that fact for me, but I have no reason to doubt its veracity.

Behind Exuma's beauty hides a history of bondage. When we Black people look into our past, we find that slavery and supremacy complicate our family stories. Lord John Rolle of England never set foot in the Caribbean, but that didn't stop him from enslaving four hundred of my ancestors. They labored uncompensated on his Exuma plantation, sending generations of fortunes back to Europe. When emancipation liberated his workforce in 1834, Lord Rolle lost interest in the Bahamas. Most freed slaves took up the surname Rolle and farmed his abandoned fields as their own.

Today, around 60 percent of the island's residents still carry the surname Rolle. I have aunties in Rolletown; my cousins Kermit and J.R. live near Rolleville. If you drive up and down Exuma's roads, you'll see a Rolle hair salon, a Rolle beauty shop, and Rolle convenience stores. Swing a stick, and you'll likely hit a Rolle somewhere in Exuma.

The pain of slavery is calcified into my family name. But in the Bahamas, the word *Rolle* has been reclaimed. Now it is spoken in joy. Part of the Black experience is to transform the slights of the past into pride. When I return to the islands and hear the name Rolle shouted from windows or see it painted in blue and yellow on signposts, I feel like a son being welcomed back to the place where my story all began.

After my belly is full of too many plates of pigeon peas 'n' rice from a friendly stove top, I make sure to visit a rocky cliff overlooking the Atlantic. On this seaside bluff sits the statue of Pompey, an enslaved warrior who led a rebellion. The figure is gold and full of muscles. Pompey is seated, spear in hand, contemplating the exact spot where slaves from Exuma were pressed into chains and forced onto ships bound for New Providence. Standing beside Pompey, I take in the same view my ancestors did as they departed for Nassau's plantations.

In 1829 Pompey commandeered one of Lord Rolle's slave ships and sailed for New Providence to fight for abolition. Slavers intercepted the ship, and to save his men, Pompey accepted thirty-nine lashes to his warrior's back. A hero's welcome awaited him on Exuma. Slaves threw down their scythes, defying their overseers' orders to work. Pompey's rebellion was a turning point in the history of Bahamian emancipation. Nine years later, a Nassau court legally ratified abolition.

When Bahamians speak of Pompey, we speak of the spirit of resiliency, of pushing boundaries, and of challenging norms as we move forward. Though we're small in number, we will not be denied. You will hear our voice—Pompey's voice. Pompey fought for the idea that the lives of Black people belong *only to us*. Liberation demands warriors; I'm ready to pick up Pompey's spiritual spear when the occasion calls for strength.

Pompey would have liked how my parents met. At eight years old, Mummy challenged Daddy to a footrace outside church. Mummy could sprint faster than most boys, and she enjoyed wearing out their shoes after Sunday service. Daddy was the only one who could keep up. I get my speed from my parents. I like to imagine them running in the sun beneath the shadow of the cross, plumes of red dust rising underfoot, each stride distancing them from the pack.

When my father was fifteen, one of his friends, shy and smitten, asked Daddy to deliver a love note and a gift to my mother. Daddy saw the opportunity to make his play. He stood on Mummy's doorstep, proclaiming, "This is from me." Daddy was a working-class kid who spent time in the country; Mummy was a well-to-do city girl. None of that stood a chance in the face of their love. They married in 1971, and my older brothers Marchant, Marvis, Mordecai, and McKinley followed in succession.

My parents wanted me to have both American and Bahamian citizenship. They had plans to move our family to America one day, and so, when my mother was seven months pregnant with me, she got permission from her ob-gyn to fly to Texas. There, she had friends from high school who took care of her in the final months of her pregnancy. On October 30, 1986, I entered this world in a delivery room in Houston. As soon as Mummy was medically able to fly, she brought me back to the islands.

Recently, Mummy showed me a picture of my baptism. Reverend Charles Saunders, whom the congregation nicknamed Shaky because of his tremors, sprinkled holy water on my tiny head at our family church, Salem Baptist in Nassau. Mummy told me that Shaky, true to form, was shaking as he held me, and she was nervous that he would drop me when baptizing me. Significantly, I began my Christian walk in the Bahamas. In the Bahamas, Christ directly informs our culture, our rules, and our social mandates. Religion is not shied away from; it's not hidden. Christ drives our social patterns. Consequently, Bahamians usually start their relationship with God in their home church. Those foundations support and extend our Christian lineage, and they set the tone for our lives.

My first memories include both the Bahamas and Christ. Even after we moved to America when I was three, my family went to the Bahamas every summer, spending half of it with Mummy's side of the family, half with Daddy's. One sunny afternoon when I was five years old, Daddy's sister Auntie Stell took my three cousins and me to a traveling fair in Nassau's Clifford Park, which is akin to New York's Central Park. Carnivals are expensive and don't show up often in the Bahamas, so you have to go when they're in town. We rode a questionably safe Ferris wheel and ate big wisps of blue cotton candy.

We were sitting on the grass as the sun was going down, stomachs aching from too much sugar, when the rain came streaming down on our heads. This was no island shower that passed quickly back into sunshine; it was a nasty squall formed over a roiling ocean that turned into a torrential downpour. Covering our heads with newspapers, we joined the fleeing crowds, heading for the safety of Auntie Stell's car. The car didn't provide much of a haven. Daddy's family didn't grow up with a whole lot of money, and Auntie Stell drove a jalopy that sputtered and puttered and gave up halfway through most trips. It didn't even have windshield wipers.

Once the engine coughed itself into motion, Auntie Stell set off stoically into the night. The rain slashed down like it had something against us. We couldn't see anything but an ever-renewing wall of water, as if we were going through an automated car wash. About a mile from the carnival, the jalopy's engine gurgled like it had a stomach full of rotten fish and died on the side of the road. On the islands, you can't call AAA, and nobody had cell phones back then. Your options were to find a pay phone and try to call a relative or abandon ship and set off on foot.

Or you can pray. Auntie Stell turned around to the frightened faces of my cousins and me and said in an even voice, "Let's pray. All of us." We started praying hard, "Please start, please start, please start." I remember clasping my hands together, looking out the scratched window at the might of the weather and hoping with all my heart that the power of God would rise against it.

Then, a sound. The engine didn't so much roar to life; it was more of an *eek*. But an *eek* was enough to get us back on the road. The night had grown the kind of dark that you get only in places without light pollution, and, of course, the car's headlights didn't work. All we could see were the black outlines of trees lining the road and the enormity of the storm. Auntie Stell opened her window, grabbed a rag, and tried to use her arm as a makeshift windshield wiper. She was wiping, wiping as water splashed into the back of the car. We were soaked, excited, terrified. Childhood magnifies everything—it felt like tsunamis were washing over us.

Auntie Stell never stopped praying. "Oh, Lord Jesus. Oh, Lord Jesus. Oh, please, Jesus. Oh, Lord," she appealed to the angry heavens as the car inched forward. She asked God for every ounce of help he could give us. And eventually, like all storms, this one subsided. Everyone in the car let out a collective gasp of, "Thank you, Lord."

Until the day she went to heaven, Auntie Stell would tell you that the car would have never made it down that dark, rainy road without God on our side. I'm inclined to agree. Collective prayer had powered the car and saved us from the wrath of the storm. Everyone in that car believed God would bring us home safely. Dripping wet, clothes muddy, we made it home together in faith. That night, I ate plates of steaming peas 'n' rice until the chill left my bones.

• • •

Though the Bahamas are a British Commonwealth, we're so close to Florida that our culture fuses with America's. You see it, you taste it, you feel it. We get American radio shows and TV shows. My uncles never missed an episode of *Miami Vice*. Bahamians will take a boat to Fort Lauderdale or Miami, shop all afternoon, then come back that night with buckets of Kentucky Fried Chicken for dinner for the whole block.

Our proximity to the States immersed Daddy's mind in the idea of the American dream. He had gotten his MBA from the University of Miami. My mother too felt we needed America's opportunities and resources to excel as young men. So when Daddy was offered a job as a systems engineer at Citibank, the Rolles moved to Galloway, New Jersey.

Daddy led the charge into American life. From the moment the Rolles set foot in Galloway, a predominantly white township twenty minutes north of Atlantic City, we focused on achievement. Mummy was the quiet type; Daddy was the hammer. They both saw enormous potential in their children and were determined not to see it wasted. Ours was a house built on framework and structure. As my brother McKinley, whom we call Cory, says, "There was no asking. There was only doing."

Daddy was a dictator, but a benevolent one. He spoke the Queen's English as properly as a royal, and he expected us boys to do the same. His distinguished mannerisms and salt-and-pepper hair reminded me, even as a child, of James Earl Jones. My father walked with an athlete's bop: he had been a sprinter and was a Bahamian national record holder in the hundred-yard dash. As he aged, football became his primary sport because he was stout and had thick, muscular legs. He's only five foot seven, but his solid base let him run through people.

Even though we were Black, and Daddy was an immigrant who spoke with a thick Bahamian accent, he was determined to push our family upward as a unit. Because we didn't have any other family around us in New Jersey, my parents beat into us, sometimes literally, the idea that we Rolles had to be our own cheerleaders. We went nowhere without the love of our family close at hand. My father never once asked me, "Myron, do you want to come watch your brother play baseball?" I just went.

Daddy never let his children make excuses and rarely praised us. If he didn't say anything to you after a football game, it meant you played well. Yet there was a softer side to him, one that showed at rare but foundational moments. I distinctly remember a day in September when I was eight, watching my brother Mordecai, whom we call Whitney, play football.

Like Mummy, Whitney was fast. He played wide receiver, and I loved the way he exploded off the line of scrimmage. The height he got when he went up for the ball made the other players look like their cleats were stuck in mud. I could tell he was grinning under his helmet. I wanted that feeling. Someday, I wanted to move like my brother did on the field.

I watched Whitney from the spot I always wiggled myself into, just below Daddy, using his legs as a cushion. For some reason that day, I put my elbows on his knees and leaned back. Daddy leaned forward and enveloped me in his arms. A soul-level warmth coursed through my chest. At that moment, I was in the safest place in the world. The protection inherent in my father's strength encircled me. A small act, perhaps, but at eight years old I understood that Daddy's presence and protection would always be with me. One day when he's no longer physically on this earth, I'll still have that feeling to wrap myself in.

Just then, Whitney caught a pass off a slant route and exploded for a thirty-yard run. Daddy shouted and cheered, still holding me in his arms. I felt the vibrations of his voice wash over me. Someday I would run like Whitney and elicit that same response from my father.

A few years ago, I told my mother about that day, about the safety I felt in Daddy's arms. "Make sure you tell your pa that," she told me.

I called him up and related the memory. "Daddy," I said, "that got to me."

When he thanked me, his voice wasn't as strong and sturdy as usual. It was lower, softer. I knew I had hit him deep. But then, as a father is apt to do, he flipped an emotional moment into a teaching one. "When you have your own children, you'll remember how that felt, and you'll do the same for them," he said.

Daddy taught me to honor my natural gifts. The greatest of those gifts was ability on the football field. Back in Nassau, Daddy helped found the Commonwealth American Football League, which was primarily composed of older athletes who put on pads once they finished working at Citibank or the Ministry of Health. They just loved football. The Miami Dolphins used to hold training camps on the islands, so there are a lot of NFL fans in the Bahamas. When we came to America, Daddy would always have football on the television on Sundays.

I started going to summer football camps in elementary school and quickly realized I was more athletically gifted than my peers. I was bigger, taller, and faster. I played more aggressively. By the time I reached fifth grade, it was clear that I stood out from the competition. I was hands down the best athlete in my grade in any sport, but I dominated in football. I'm not saying that to brag, it was a simple matter of fact. A substantial gap existed between me and anyone my age.

The question for my family was: What should we do with that talent? My parents and my older brothers saw that my ability made the idea of playing in the National Football League more than a pipe dream. They believed in the possibility of that vision and helped me develop the skills I would need to make it happen. Together we went to work.

Daddy would take me out in the mornings before school and train on the beach in Atlantic City. After long days at the office, Daddy would take Cory and me to the track to run sprints. As my lungs burned, I would hear his words in my ears: "Be so good that they can't deny you."

Daddy took me through drills like I was at two-a-days. I practiced staying low throughout my backpedal, then planting my feet and driving through tackles. After dinner, I'd walk through the house with a football, and my brothers would try to knock it out of my hands while I held on to it tightly. We watched NFL legends like Rod Woodson, Deion Sanders, Darrell Green, and my cousin, Samari Rolle. I studied how they competed on the field and how they tackled with their heads up, smashing through a player.

My brothers picked up where Daddy left off. My oldest brother, Marchant, was fifteen years older than I was. He mentored me, old enough to be as strict as Daddy when it came to school and athletics but hip enough to take me to my first Prince concert. He studied at Penn State while I was growing up, and one time he took me to a dance thrown by the Caribbean Student Association. I remember grooving to reggae, the youngest kid on the dance floor.

Marvis—I call him Rahlu—was the most athletic of all of us. He could jump out of the gym, just nasty in terms of raw athleticism. He is also the kindest of the Rolles. He will give everything he has to make sure you're okay. Growing up, I would say to him, "Hey, Rahlu, I want to work on my footwork," after he had come from a long night of working or being out with his friends. Even though he was tired, even though his body was hurting, he would still go and work out with me. Then he would take me to McDonald's, buy me everything I wanted, and take me home.

Whitney educated me about everything that surrounds football. He taught me about swag, how to deal with women, and how to deal with bullies. Haters were not to be dwelled on—they were albatrosses to ascension. I remember Whitney's brolic figure standing over me anytime I had a problem, saying, "Look up, Myron, look up. You are beyond this. This is insignificant when it comes to where you are going and the man you are going to be." Whitney was adamant that I never touch alcohol and didn't stay out past curfew with the wrong crowd. I didn't feel imprisoned by his rule book—it gave me a blueprint for how to live like the man I wanted to become. He made me realize there were steps I needed to take *now* to achieve a bigger goal down the line.

Cory was two years older than I was. We're just alike—Mummy and Daddy treated us as twins. We shared the same bunk bed and showered together as kids. He would stand in the front of the shower facing the showerhead, and I would be on the other side, behind him, with my back to him, and then we'd flip. Mummy called it Bahamian style.

Cory and I went everywhere as a pod. I rocked a Charlotte Hornets jacket; Cory sported a similar Georgetown Hoyas jacket.

I had a Pittsburgh Steelers shirt; he had a similar Dallas Cowboys shirt. Same design, different teams. We loved each other as hard as we competed against each other. On weekends, Whitney liked to grease up Cory and me and have us box in the living room. We would really go after it, throwing blows until one of the older brothers had to break it up. No matter how hard we fought, both of our noses remained unbroken. Rolles don't cheap-shot one another.

● ● ●

Though I was a gifted student and athlete, I still struggled with my identity throughout my youth. My report card and rushing stats didn't reflect the turmoil I felt inside. Fights were not uncommon. Neither were suspensions. Marchant told me not to give my haters attention, but my blood rushed red, and my fists often flew.

A white boy in my grade, whom I'll call Kevin, liked to push my buttons. One afternoon, as the yellow bus carried us back from school, we argued over a subject I can no longer recall. He sat a few rows ahead of me and lobbed insults at me over his shoulder. I fired right back.

Right before the bus reached his stop, Kevin turned in his seat and said, "Yeah, well, your momma is a b——, and you're a n——."

I got red-hot; my fists formed into tight hammers. The screech of rusty bus brakes sounded, followed by the whoosh of the doors. "You better run!" a chorus of children screamed. Good advice.

Kevin jetted for the exit. He must have known he wouldn't get far—I was the fastest kid in our school by a mile. I was on him before the bus pulled away. I grabbed him with my left hand and hauled off on him with my right. A few more rapid shots to the body and head sent him to the pavement.

I felt sturdy arms wrap around me. "He's done," Cory told me. "Let's get out of here."

This wasn't our stop—we had ground to cover before we reached the safety of the Rolle household. As we sprinted past suburban lawns, Cory looked over his shoulder. A minivan followed behind us.

We went inside our house, rushing past Daddy into our bedroom, and crouched beside a dresser. A few seconds later, someone pounded on our door. I heard the latch turn, and then the house erupted in screaming.

"Your son just beat up my son!" a woman's voice rang out. "He's a menace."

"Don't you come into my house and insult my family," Daddy countered. "My boys are good boys. What right do you have?"

"I'm taking you to court," Kevin's mother said. "You won't get away with this."

The door slammed shut. Heavy footsteps thumped toward our room. Cory and I looked at each other, expecting wrath. Daddy's silhouette appeared in the doorway. He crouched down, getting his face even with ours.

"I protect you because you are my sons," he said. "But you have some serious explaining to do."

When Daddy heard that Kevin had called me a racial slur and his wife a name that was never uttered in our household, he nodded slowly. I get my temper from my father—he would have done the same thing in my situation.

Kevin's mother made good on her heated promise. We received a summons from the Atlantic City courthouse a few weeks later. The morning of my court date, Mummy woke me up. She stood over my bed holding my only suit on a hanger.

"Myron," she said. "Next time I see you wear this suit, it will be in church, not in court."

"Yes, Mummy," I said, my eyes searching the floor.

My parents had engaged the services of a lawyer, a Black woman who told me to call her Miss Fauntleroy. Her short haircut and smart suit made her look like she lived in New York City. Before we went inside the courthouse, she took me aside.

"You're only ten years old," Miss Fauntleroy said. "That is not going to be the last time you hear that word from a white person."

"It's not right," I said, feeling a bone-deep anger throb through me.

"You and I both know that. But this is the world we live in. We have to find a way to excel in it. If you end up in court every time you hear that word, you and I are going to see far too much of each other. You're a smart kid. You've got a lot going for you. But it's how you respond to these things that makes you a man."

"But I'm not a man yet," I said.

"Black boys have to grow up fast," she said. "Let's go get this over with."

Inside the courthouse, I stood in front of Kevin and his family and explained myself to the judge. As I shared that I had straight A's and played four sports, my gaze shifted toward my parents. Daddy's face held no clue to his feelings. Mummy sat with her shoulders tight, as if she were at a funeral. An emotion I had never seen before played across her face: disappointment.

I knew what she was thinking. She'd left her family and friends in the Bahamas, all that she knew and loved, to give her son a better life. Now her youngest, her "last pain" as she sometimes called me, was standing in his church suit in front of a judge. Would this outburst destroy all the dreams she had dreamed for me?

I braced myself for punishment. The judge lectured me about the futility of violence but said if I apologized to Kevin and his family, I was free to go. Relief rippled across Mummy's face. Her son's promise was still intact.

On the car ride home, Daddy finally spoke. "I understand why you hit that boy," he said. "But it's time for you to be responsible for your actions. Don't let others dictate your future." His voice wasn't angry, it was solemn.

The consequence of my carelessness crashed over me. I never wanted to see that look on Mummy's face or hear that tone in

Daddy's voice ever again. I resolved to leave behind my temper. Anger would only impede my progress.

It's no coincidence that only a few weeks later, I formally gave my life to Christ. I remember the day I got saved, April 19, 1998. Sitting in church, wearing the same suit I had in court, I heard our pastor, an older white man named Pastor Bult, ask, "If you died today, where would your spirit go?" He asked the question matter-of-factly. He didn't use any colorful language. There was no follow-up.

As I sat in the pew, I said to myself, "I don't know."

I knew I loved Christ. I'd been baptized, and I went to church every Sunday. But I didn't know the answer to Pastor Bult's question. I knew only that I was scared of the uncertainty of what lay beyond death.

Then, as if he was speaking directly to me, Pastor Bult said, "If you don't know that answer, I want you to come forward here to the altar, and we can help." I thought, "This is my time. If I get out of my seat and step into the middle of the aisle, I could walk toward Christ."

When I stood, Pastor Bult's face broke into joy. He put out his hand, waving me on. People started crying in the pews. It's not typical that a young person walks to the altar in front of the whole congregation. I wanted to make a bold move, like Pompey would have done.

One of the deacons grabbed me and hugged me. He asked me, "Are you willing to die today and to be reborn in Christ?"

"I am," I replied.

I didn't feel like some sort of power came over me. But I did feel different, accountable. I was more responsible for my actions and for how I treated other people. As time went on and my friends at school—except my best friend, Ryan Roman—began skipping class, smoking weed, and drinking, I felt a natural aversion. The attraction to those things had died, but it was confusing because I still felt like maybe I should experience them. I tried to wrap my young head around how I was changing, but I kept running into a fog.

One night, I paced around my room, wrestling with these thoughts. I went downstairs to where Daddy was sitting on the couch watching the evening news. Blue light flickered on his face.

"Daddy, can I talk to you?" I asked.

He patted the couch, and I sat down next to him.

"I don't know what's going on with me," I told him. "I have all these questions I never thought about before."

"What kinds of questions?"

"What do I do when people ask me to cheat on a test with them? Or skip school?" I asked, speaking rapidly, the words pouring out of me. "I know I don't want to do these things, but I feel like I'm being pulled in two different directions."

"Myron," he said, "you've got Christ in your life right now, and he should remain there. You're becoming a man, and this is a part of manhood."

"It's hard to tell people no. But when I think of these things, you and Mummy spring to my mind."

"You're starting to make decisions for yourself and the people around you," Daddy replied.

"I want to help people, I know that."

"Good decisions put you in the position to succeed. But they're also going to help other people around you move forward. You know your life is not your own. You're becoming a leader. This is what leaders do."

His words cut through my mishmash of emotions. *This is what leaders do*. Swirling thoughts became a clear line of purpose. I needed to walk with faith and with confidence. It was a blessed assurance to know there wasn't something wrong with me. I no longer doubted the man I needed to be, the leader my family and community were hoping I would become.

My attitude changed. No more suspensions. No more fights in the schoolyard. I got involved in extracurriculars like "Brain Brawl" scholar competitions. I wrote for our school newspaper and learned how to play the baritone saxophone. I blew jazz tunes for seniors at our local nursing home. I couldn't have cared less that my schoolmates were smoking weed under the Atlantic City pier. Now that I saw the road I was meant to walk, each step was easier to take.

• • •

The summer after I gave my life to Christ, I was sitting in the living room watching ESPN when the front door swung open and Marchant strutted into the house.

"Catch," he said, tossing me a book.

I snatched it out of the air and read the cover. *Gifted Hands: The Ben Carson Story.*

"You'll dig it," Marchant told me.

I tore through the pages. Dr. Carson had come from the streets of Detroit to the halls of Johns Hopkins Hospital in Baltimore, where he had become the head of pediatric neurosurgery at the age of thirty-three. Like me, he had a family who focused on education. He had a temper; he felt both sure of his identity and confronted by those who wanted him to fit into a box that didn't fit him. In Dr. Carson's story, I recognized the boy I saw in the mirror and saw a model for the kind of man I wanted to become.

When Mummy called me down to the dinner table that night, I still had the book in my hands. Long after the rest of the family went to bed, I sat up turning pages. One passage leveled me. "I became acutely aware of an unusual ability—a divine gift, I believe—of extraordinary eye and hand coordination," Dr. Carson wrote. "It's my belief that God gives us all gifts, special abilities that we have the privilege of developing to help us serve Him and humanity."[1]

I knew then that I wanted to be a surgeon. That dream ignited a similar fire in me as football did. The part of me that wanted to say, "I'm going to Disney World as the Super Bowl MVP," was equivalent to my desire to operate on somebody's brain. I wanted to be Deion "Prime Time" Sanders *and* Ben Carson.

I got up from my bed and went searching for a notebook. I opened a page and wrote in big block letters.

When you grow up . . .

1. Play football in the NFL
2. Become a neurosurgeon

It wouldn't be easy to become a professional football player *and* a neurosurgeon. But from that day forth, I inched toward both of those paths, academia and athletics, without reservation. These dreams could become realities if I honored the talent God had given me. Of course, at that age, I had no idea how much of myself and my soul that journey would ultimately require or how many people would try to say my dreams were impossible.

● ● ●

Though it wasn't a democracy, our family was grounded in love as much as it was in achievement. Mummy was the source of that love. If I scored only one touchdown in a football game, Daddy would be silent, but Mummy would tell me I'd played the best game she'd ever seen in her life.

One day when I was in middle school, my father's car pulled up to the house earlier than usual. I heard my parents whispering in the hallway. Their words were thick with worry.

Citibank had laid Daddy off. Life changed quickly. We moved from our four-bedroom house in the white-picket-fence suburbs to a two-bedroom town house in the worst part of town. Quarters were tight, and sometimes the water ran cold from the showerhead.

One day Daddy left with the family car and came home driving a '96 Ford Taurus.

"It's silver," Mummy said. "Silver is a great color."

Mummy started working three jobs. After a shift at the Trump Plaza Hotel and Casino in Atlantic City, she'd head directly to the Showboat casino for another six hours. On weekends, she rang up customers at a Sears in our local mall. She still somehow found the time to cook, drive my brothers and me to football practice, cut our hair, and sign permission slips for field trips we could not afford.

At the time, I wasn't conscious of how poor we were. When our lights were shut off, I went outside and reread *Gifted Hands* under the glow of a streetlamp. I told myself that cold showers were fun because they were quick. I liked my hand-me-downs because my brothers had worn them. I didn't mind praying with Mummy for our car to start because I remembered when Auntie Stell had gotten me home in a jalopy that rumbled more than our Taurus.

But as the months turned to years, I became more aware of our socioeconomic status. One day, toward the end of middle school, Mummy drove me, as she always did, to one of my Little League games. I played outfield, outfitted in Whitney's old cleats and using Rahlu's glove, and ran to catch a fly ball. "Easy out," I thought. As I jumped, I felt a snap. My cleat had broken.

I collapsed into the grass, watching the runner round the bases. I saw the other team cheering in their dugout, but I wasn't focused on their faces. I saw their shiny new bats, their well-oiled gloves, their new Nike cleats. As I got up, picked up the ball, and hurled it to the shortstop, the shame of poverty washed over me. I kept my composure during the ride home, but when I walked through the door, I began to cry.

"Myron, what's wrong?" Mummy asked, drawing me to her chest.

"I got holes in my shoes, Mummy."

"I know, baby, I know."

"I don't want to live in this house anymore," I said. "I want . . ."

"Shhh . . .," she said, running her hands down the small of my neck. "It's okay, baby. All this crying is doing us no good. Calm down and go tell your father exactly what you just told me."

I found my way to my parents' bedroom. Daddy sat on the edge of the bed, leafing through a leather portfolio.

"What's that, Daddy?" I asked.

"Résumés," he said without looking up.

Another sob found its way into my throat. Daddy's eyes snapped toward me. He stood and moved toward me. "Tell me," he said.

I was scared, but Mummy's instructions rang in my mind. I told him how I felt. He was silent but embraced me. In his arms I had the same feeling I had between his knees on the football bleachers. *Safety. Everything was going to be okay.* Two weeks later, Daddy found a new job. Within a couple of months, we moved from that two-bedroom town house into a five-bedroom standalone house with a pool and a backyard. Next baseball season, I laced up a new pair of cleats.

Mummy's resilience is the essence of the 2% Way, both in terms of practice and purpose. For an immigrant woman with no college degree, losing her family's primary source of income must have been daunting. Instead of letting the weight of the situation overwhelm her, she used each day to carry a small piece of it. Every smoky casino shift she worked was 2 percent more money for school supplies. Every time she supported my father was an encouragement to him to get 2 percent closer to finding a new job.

Mummy had built a strong version of herself, and a vision for her family, that couldn't be torn apart by adversity. She hung tough because she knew her life was not her own; it belonged to her husband and her sons. Each small step she took was for us. And when the time was right, we'd gladly walk for her.

Chapter 2

IMAGE AND PRIVILEGE

By the time I turned thirteen, I could run a forty-yard dash in under five seconds and had a good twenty pounds of muscle on all my peers, and my report card was A's down the line. These specs made me a shoo-in for a scholarship to the prep school of my choice. My family wanted to place me somewhere close to Galloway that offered the right balance of competitive academics and sports. We ended up deciding on the Peddie School, a boarding academy in Hightstown, New Jersey.

Peddie's campus was immaculate—mature leafy trees towered over stately stone-and-brick buildings and manicured lawns. Peddie boasted four soccer fields, two football fields, two field hockey fields, four lacrosse fields, two baseball diamonds, a softball field, ten tennis courts, and an eighteen-hole golf course on the grounds. I'd never even been to a driving range.

On the first day of school, Daddy dropped me off in our 1996 silver Ford Taurus, while my classmates climbed out of Range Rovers and Benzes. At first I thought these cars belonged to their parents. Then I watched a girl park a sparkling forest green Jaguar fresh off the lot and heard her tell a friend it was a sweet sixteen gift. She pouted with mock disappointment; she had asked for a Porsche. A

Bentley pulled up next, piloted by a chauffeur in a felt driving cap. Peddie's black iron gate, emblazoned with the school's seal engraved with the words *Finimus Pariter Renovamusque Labores*—Latin for "When we finish our labors, we begin them anew"—swung open, and my Air Jordans stepped into a world of penny loafers and English riding boots.

Most students at Peddie suffered from a condition I call affluenza. Affluenza seeped into the way my classmates walked through Peddie's halls. They floated with a confidence that was the polar opposite of my brothers' earned swagger. Each careless step proclaimed, *This education is my birthright*. In many ways, it was. Their parents walked the same way.

Their entitlement stemmed from knowing no other world than the one where things always went their way. They were blind to the hidden mechanisms of privilege that had *bestowed* their place in the world. But those forces were not invisible to me, and watching how they functioned made me keenly aware that my presence at this institution would not automatically confer those benefits.

In fact, these forces were a threat to my progress, my dignity, and even my safety. Not only could my daddy not write a check to paper over my mistakes, but someone else's daddy might use his influence to create trouble for the out-of-town football player whom he suspected had eyes for his daughter. I became hyperaware of every aspect of my social interactions as if I were evading tackles. Actually, they were more troublesome than high school defenses. Linebackers I could juke. I still haven't figured out how to outmaneuver institutional power.

I became aware of this social imbalance as I scouted the dormitory halls on move-in day. A few doors down from me, a boy named Ryan was moving in with his parents. His dad, who worked at a hedge fund in New York City, had slicked-back hair and wore a blue blazer over an unbuttoned white oxford shirt to show a tuft of chest hair. The mom was thin enough to blow away in the wind, and you could tell she'd had more than a few Botox injections in her face. Diamonds clung to wrists and neck, and she smelled like I imagined Elizabeth Taylor might as she walked down the red carpet. The whole family wore sunglasses inside.

Ryan and his father were carrying a huge flat-screen television into his room. My first, naive thought was, "That would be a dope TV to watch Monday Night Football on." Then I heard the mother's voice. "Do you go here?"

Something hot grew in my chest. The burning traveled to my throat, and had I opened my mouth, I would have said, "Yeah, b—, I go here. Why else would I be in this dorm?"

Two things kept my mouth shut: my religion and my skin color. Every Black kid grows up with enough common sense to know that calling a white woman a b— on your first day of school means that it will also be your last day of school. I looked at this woman and managed to force out the words, "Yes, ma'am." I tried to look her in the eyes, but her oversized Gucci frames shielded them.

Her thin lips pursed into a *hmm*. She removed her glasses and gave her husband a look that said, *I can't believe they invite these kinds of people to a school like this.* Then she looked at Ryan and, with a glance, directed his attention toward the television. *Stay away from this kid, and watch your things*, her cocked eyebrow silently warned.

As I walked away, confusion rattled my head. "Did that just happen?" I asked myself. I busted out of the dorm's doors and sat on the sidewalk, replaying the scene in my head. I wanted that moment back. I imagined myself planting my stance, jutting my chin out, and saying, "Yes, I go here. I'm here on an academic and football scholarship. And I'm going to get better grades than your son. And, if I felt like it, I could put him, his daddy, and that flat-screen TV through the wall with one move of my shoulder."

My mind played out that fantasy for ten angry minutes. Then I said to myself, "You know what? That moment is lost. It's gone. I can't change what happened." I walked back inside, steadying my resolve against all that I knew was to come. In that steadiness, I felt a certain control over myself, which was all the control I would be afforded in a place where I was viewed as an interloper. For the time being, that was enough.

Though I hadn't yet learned about the 2% Way, I realized that improving myself by focusing on my core values and beliefs was more important than trying to fit in at Peddie or fixating on my classmates' constant microaggressions. My skill on the football field gave me confidence in my identity. I was a Black man imbued with God-given intelligence, drive, and physical gifts. This world might not accept me, but they could not deny me. My Christianity gave me the strength and courage of conviction to say, "Yes, ma'am," to that woman and refrain from reacting in a way that would have been detrimental to my future.

I steered clear of Ryan during my two years at Peddie. I never wanted to feel like that again. This may have been petty of me, but from that day forth, I saw every parent and entitled white kid at that school as potential impediments to my future, rather than friends. I put many of them in a bucket labeled *dangerous* before they had a chance to dismiss me or point an accusatory finger in my direction. Perhaps I should have given more people a chance, but I was worried that one misunderstanding would jeopardize my future, or worse.

"Myron, you don't ever let your guard down," Cory observed when I called him one Friday night to tell him I was, once again, watching a football game alone.

"Why don't I?" I pondered.

"Because you know better than that," he replied.

Though I was only fourteen, I *did* know better than that. In every social stratum of America, people of color are forced to carefully negotiate a dizzying maze of social rules and prejudices at an age when we should just be figuring ourselves out. We choose the path of safety because one wrong move can spell disaster. We protect ourselves because we must. The person we are when we are alone, or with each other, and the person we must become in predominantly white spaces become two splintered sides of ourselves. One is a necessity, the other a relief.

Thankfully, my roommate, Colin, was an open-minded kid. He had long, curly, bright red hair, and we watched *Chappelle's Show* together on the DVDs his parents sent him. Colin got into reggae music by osmosis from my CD collection. When we'd see each other on campus, we'd riff on Buju Banton and Beenie Man lines.

"How do *you* know reggae?" a girl chimed in one afternoon after economics class.

"Don' worry about it, ma, don' worry about it," Colin replied in a terrible impersonation of patois. He was wearing pink pants covered in lime-green Polo logos, Birkenstock sandals, and aviator glasses. I thought, "I don't remember them speaking patois in Abercrombie & Fitch commercials."

Thankfully, Colin had enough sense not to get white-boy braids, or I might have had to find a new roommate. Though we got along, our friendship remained surface level. The difference in our socioeconomic status divided us, and I kept my guard up around him. My mantra was "Not one mistake, not ever."

So, as has often happened in my life, I took refuge in the friendship of a Black woman. Bridgette Mitchell was six foot one and a *dog* on the basketball court. The first time I saw her punish some poor opponent in the paint, I thought, "Oh, I like her grit." She took no prisoners, and from the first whistle to the last, she was out for blood and enjoyed getting it. I saw in her the same sort of fire for basketball I had for football—I knew we'd vibe.

Like the majority of the Black students at Peddie, both Bridgette and I were on scholarships. We had to be on our best behavior, or the funding for our education would be yanked. In private, walking along the shore of Peddie Lake in the evenings, watching the rowing crews glide across the surface in their long black boats, Bridgette had no qualms about telling me what was on her mind, often at high volume. She cracked on my gear. If I had a scuff on my Timberlands, she would tell me, "Myron, those Tims are wack." If my haircut wasn't quite right, she would say, "Boy, you better get shaped up because you're looking trash." I loved her for the raw honesty of her pure, genuine personality. We could be ourselves around each other, unbothered by the complex intricacies that restrained our social interactions with other peers. I could relax and be myself for a few precious minutes.

Bridgette got her rawness from growing up on a hard block in Trenton, New Jersey. There's a bridge in Trenton that says, "What Trenton makes, the world takes." Trenton used to be an industrial town. The world rolled into Trenton in eighteen-wheeler container trucks to haul away goods and left crime, dysfunctional families, and broken school systems behind. Galloway wasn't as tough as Trenton, but Bridgette and I shared the fact that we were at Peddie when we were not *supposed* to be there. Not supposed to be succeeding in the classroom. Not supposed to be at formal dinners eating lobster thermidor with trust-funders.

Bridgette and I were lucky to find each other. Sometimes, I felt like she was all I had. At school dances, we'd groove only with each other because—let's be honest—white prep school kids can't dance. Together, moving as one, we created a little bubble of joy. We knew we looked good.

I thought I would form tight bonds with more Black students at Peddie because there were so few of us. But those relationships carried their own fraught dynamics, which, on one occasion, devolved into violence. Peddie's top brass had made a weak attempt to increase diversity by admitting a few Black kids from Newark and New York City through a minority inclusion program. These kids stuck together, forming a clique called D-Block. They stole their name from Sheek Louch, Styles P, and Jadakiss's rap group, whose hit "Ryde or Die" blasted from their car stereos.

D-Block acted as if they were as hard as Bronx concrete, and the white boys at school marveled at their personas. These city kids were savvy enough to realize that most Peddie students had only seen Black people in rap music videos, and they embraced that image to seem tough to kids with pink polo sweaters tied around their shoulders. But they didn't have me fooled. I knew if these boys showed up with that act at Atlantic City High School, twenty minutes from where I grew up, or fronted like that in the Bahamas, they would be called out immediately. You can't be in a hard gangster group at a boarding school. It's simply not possible to be hood when you're sitting down to a formal dinner with two salad forks and a soup course every Tuesday night.

I caught a lot of heat from D-Block at the lunch table. Part of being a young Black person means if somebody jokes on you, you have to laugh it off and come back with some fire lines. You have to take it, and you have to dish it. The more quick-witted, the better. You can't be too sensitive, but everyone knows where the line is. D-Block were habitual line-steppers. Unfortunately, perhaps because of internalized racism, these kids had a "crabs in a barrel" mentality. If they saw another Black person succeeding, instead of, as we say in the Bahamas, "bigging him up" by praising and celebrating him, they wanted to tear him down to their level. They liked to play this game where they kissed their hand, licked their palm, and smacked somebody's head as hard as they could. It was supposed to be playful and joking, but these guys teetered on the edge of maliciousness.

One day I walked into the lunchroom with a fresh haircut, a nice bald fade. I started eating alone, as I usually did when Bridgette was away hooping. A boy named Lamar broke away from D-Block and moved toward me. I didn't see him, but I heard the kissing of the hand, the licking of the palm, a sound like a baseball whizzing by my head, and then a *boom* in my ears.

The slap was so loud that everyone in the lunchroom audibly

inhaled. Blood rushed to the skin of my newly shaved scalp. I looked back, hands covering my smarting skull, to see if another blow was on its way. Through my blurred vision, I saw Lamar skipping back toward D-Block, laughing. That set me off. The pain I could take; the disrespect I had to address.

Though I had barely touched my food, I got up and threw my lunch in the trash without uttering a syllable. D-Block chirped away as I stalked off. It took all my self-control not to go and body-slam that little boy in the lunchroom in front of all our teachers.

Back in my dorm, I dropped into push-up position. I pounded out fifty. Still mad. I began shadowboxing, picturing Lamar's face in front of my fists. I paced back and forth in my room, but the anger remained. I said to myself, "I'm going to light this punk up."

Even with my spirit on fire, my father's face swam into my mind. I thought about what his eyes would look like if I had to face him after getting kicked out of school. Yet I couldn't let this trespass go unpunished—Pompey certainly wouldn't have. I whipped out my Nokia, dialed my dad's number, and explained the situation. He listened quietly, as he always does.

"Daddy, can I go and beat him up?" I asked when I finished.

"Myron, put the phone down right now, and go handle your business."

I said, "That's it." I hit End on that phone and waged a warpath to Lamar's dorm. All the D-Block boys were hanging out in the hallway. They saw the fumes coming out of my head and let me walk right past. I wasn't worried about them. I knew they were not about that life.

I banged on the door. "Lamar, you coming out, or am I coming in?"

Lamar appeared, looking sheepish. I grabbed him by the shirt, picked him up, and threw him into the dorm's cinder block wall. His head hit the wall with a *bop*. I used his momentum to take him down, bouncing his skull off the floor. Today, as a neurosurgeon, if I saw someone's head smack the wall and floor as Lamar's did, I would test him for a concussion. Twice.

Lamar got in one limp punch before I started laying into him. Right, left, right, left, right, left, right, left. I kept going. When he was almost unconscious, his boys pulled me off him. I turned to D-Block and said, "You all want some more? I'm right here. You all know who I am."

That night, Daddy drove two hours in his trusty Ford Taurus from Galloway, and Cory took a bus from Queens, New York, to make sure I had reinforcements if D-Block called their real hood friends to jump me. Daddy looked me in the eyes to make sure I was okay and told me that he would always be there if anything like this happened again.

The only fallout, thankfully, was a stern talking-to by Dean Samuel Tattersall. Lamar and I were both Black boys. If I'd tuned up one of the white kids whose parents had donated a wing, I would have been on the first bus back to Galloway or, more likely, to Northern State Prison in Newark. Gone. You would have never heard the name Myron Rolle.

That was the only fight I ever got into at Peddie. I focused on punishing people on the football field. During my freshman year, I started on offense and defense, was arguably the best player on my team, and won all-conference. I burst onto the scene like gangbusters, and local publications started writing about me.

In the off-season, my brother Cory acted like my de facto agent. He told me, "Look, you're good against most of these prep school kids, but let's see how you do nationally." The University of Oklahoma was hosting a football camp in Norman, Oklahoma, that summer. The university was ranked number one nationally, led by head coach Bob Stoops. They had beaten Florida State in the national championship the year before.

My parents rented a white van from a shifty dealership in Absecon called Just Four Wheels. We packed up and drove nearly twenty-four hours straight to Norman. I showed up wearing my brother Whitney's hand-me-down jersey. Whitney sported number three, and it turned out to be a lucky number for me.

I started out with a freshman and sophomore group. There was a junior and senior group that was getting more attention from the Oklahoma football coaches—these were the guys the coaches were likely going to give scholarships to. A guy named Reggie Smith—a defensive back from Santa Fe High School in Edmond, Oklahoma— was the five-star hotshot recruit there. Everyone wanted him. Reggie was one hundred ninety pounds of fast-twitch muscle who would eventually be drafted seventy-fifth overall by the San Francisco 49ers after a distinguished career at Oklahoma. All the coaches hovered around him, asking, "Reggie, how you doing, Reg? Hey, Reg. What's up, Reg?" I was at the back of the line. They didn't know me from Adam.

I thought, "How do I get the love that Reggie Smith is getting right now?" I decided I was just going to go out there and ball. Go play my game, do what I do. And so, when I went with the freshmen and sophomores doing drills against each other, I started destroying these guys. When we ran backpedaling drills, my technique was smooth and fluid. My body remembered the hours spent perfecting my timing with Whitney back when I was in fourth and fifth grade. I batted every ball thrown my way. I hit players like I meant it. I started to feel myself. I was balling against these Oklahoma boys.

That's when I heard the chatter. A buzz rose through the ranks of the coaching staff. *Who is this kid?* Oklahoma's defensive coordinator, Mike Stoops, asked one of the local reporters, a guy named Jeremy Crabtree, who wrote for a site called Rivals.com, which ranked high school players, to get the scoop about me.

"Hey, what's your name?" he asked.

"I'm Myron Rolle."

"Where are you from?"

"Jersey, sir."

"Aw, man. Jersey. Why are you here?"

"My father is a big Oklahoma fan," I said. "We thought we'd try out and see what I could do out here."

Crabtree snapped my picture. A few minutes later, Mike Stoops came over and said, "You Jersey boys, you can play a little bit of ball, huh? What year are you?"

"Freshman, sir."

"Okay, Jersey boy. Move to my group."

I dominated that group too, a one-man wrecking crew. Nobody could catch a ball against me, I intercepted almost every pass, and I was knocking dudes cold. After a play where I locked up a tight end who was supposed to be hot stuff, I heard a voice say, "Hey, Rolle, come over here." I looked up and saw Bob Stoops, the head coach and Sooner legend, standing in the middle of the field calling *my* name. Stoops was a football god in Oklahoma. To get a whiff of attention from him was amazing. I trotted over to him, suppressing the urge to sprint.

"Are you here by yourself?" Stoops asked me, peering at me from under his white Sooners visor.

I told him I drove from Jersey with my parents.

"How long did that take?"

"About twenty-four hours, sir."

"You must really want to be out here."

"Yes, sir, I do."

"Let's go say hello to your parents." Stoops walked me toward Mummy and Daddy on the sidelines.

"Mrs. Rolle, Mr. Rolle, your son is an outstanding player," he said when we reached them. "I want to invite you guys up to my office after this session. Do you have a change of clothes, Myron?"

Luckily, I always had a pair of nice clothes with me. It's a Bahamian thing—you have to be ready to look presentable at a moment's notice. In the family van, I buttoned up my shirt, spritzed on some cologne, and went with my parents to Coach Stoops's office.

I glanced at the *Sports Illustrated* cover of Oklahoma's perfect 2000 season on the shelf behind his desk. The polished wood paneling reminded me of Peddie, with one fundamental difference. Here I would be accorded the respect I had earned. Bob Stoops treated players like the men we were.

After Coach Stoops let me try on all his National Championship rings, he sat me down on the edge of his desk and said, "Son, I'm going to offer you a full football scholarship to the University of Oklahoma. I've never offered a scholarship to anyone as young as you since Rod Woodson." To be mentioned in the same breath as a Hall of Fame defensive back validated all the sacrifices I had made to get to this point in my life.

It was important to me that my parents were able to witness that moment of validation. It was validation for them too. They were fired up. As soon as we got back to the hotel, they started calling family back in the Bahamas, bragging on me. They had always thought I had a shot at this dream, but now it was real. *I* was for real.

I finished the camp on cloud nine. The rumor got out that I had been offered a scholarship. All the guys crowded me, asking, "Oh, man, what's Stoops like? Did he offer you a new car?" Jeremy Crabtree wrote an article about me dominating and blowing up the Oklahoma football camp. I was this kid nobody knew about the day before, but that article announced my arrival on the national scene. On that summer day, I came out of nowhere to become one of the hottest high school recruits in the country.

● ● ●

I transferred to the Hun School of Princeton after my sophomore year to further my football career. Hun's coach and I saw more eye to eye on my future than Peddie's and I did. The change of scenery didn't change my attitude toward prep school life. I assumed the students there would suffer from the same affluenza as Peddie's, and they proved me right. I knew what it was like to miss meals or not have enough money to pay my bills. If you come from a Caribbean country, prep school kids think you live in a grass shack and walk around without any shoes. If you're a Black jock, the respect you earn on the gridiron is not granted to you when you walk off the field. I felt typecast and stereotyped into a box that I would never fit into.

But I kept my head up, like my brother Whitney always told me to. I was there to play football and to take advantage of what Hun had to offer. It was a learning experience, one where I used the skills I had learned in football to excel beyond the field. There were formal dinners where I learned etiquette on how to correctly use a knife and fork, how to converse in a formal setting, and how to conduct myself in high society. Some of Hun's classes employed the Harkness method, where students sat around a large table, discussing deep ideas and abstract concepts. We spoke on Henry David Thoreau and *Walden*, the aftermath of September 11, and the ramifications of the invasion of privacy written into the Patriot Act. I valued the depth of knowledge I was steadily accruing.

Extracurricular activities, like student government, student speeches in the chapel, and Habitat for Humanity, where I built homes in West Virginia and Florida, broadened me and gave me a deeper understanding of the important cultural and political issues of the day. I sang and acted in the school musical as Tevye in *Fiddler on the Roof*: a white Russian Jewish milkman with five white daughters. The role was an opportunity to break the stereotypes of being a Black football player. On top of all this, I maintained a 4.0 GPA and accumulated twenty-one advanced placement credits toward college.

I did take one more stab at prep school social life. A white baseball player invited me over to a party in the basement to watch *Bad Boys II*. I thought, "I'll give it a shot." When I got there, everyone was playing beer pong. I'd never drunk in my life but wanted to see Will Smith drive that silver Lambo in South Beach.

There's a scene in the movie where Will Smith shoots a Haitian drug dealer in the head. The baseball player stood up, spilling his beer on his pants, and yelled at the screen, "Shoot that n——. That's right. Shoot that n——."

Suddenly, the only sound in the room was Martin Lawrence's booming laugh. Everyone stared at me, mouths agape. Fear shone in their eyes, as if I was going to pull out a gun like Will Smith and light up the room. All I wanted to do was get out of there.

Then the dam holding back all their white guilt broke. Some of the partygoers demanded the ball player apologize; he did nothing but cower in the corner of the room. A group of girls swarmed me, asking, "Oh my gosh, Myron. Are you okay?" They tried to hug me. The last thing I wanted was to be touched. After that, I didn't go to parties anymore. My lack of a social life no longer bothered me. Everyone said I should try to be like a normal high school kid, but if that was normalcy, I didn't want any part of it.

Something that *did* bother me was the level of surveillance I felt I was under from Hun's faculty. They would come around to check that my work was finished, inspect my room to make sure it was clean, and examine my internet history to make sure I wasn't going to any prohibited sites. Their monitoring made me feel as if I were a problem kid, as if I had behavioral issues, as if I were destined to fail at their elite school. Of course, the racial irony is that I was the epitome of what they wanted a Hun student to be.

I was so fed up with the surveillance, with the disengagement that I felt in my social spheres, and with white kids saying the N-word in front of me that I snapped one night. I called my brother Cory up at St. John's University in Queens, New York, after midnight. "I have to get out of this school," I told him. "Can I come see you?"

"Don't leave, man," he said, alert and attuned to my suffering. "You're the number one high school player in the country. You've got scholarships. Everybody wants you. It wouldn't be a good look to leave." He talked me off the ledge. The next morning, Cory took the train down to see me and spent the day with me. His presence and advice comforted me, as only an older brother can.

I doubled down on academics and football. By my senior year, I was a high school All-American. ESPN ranked me the number one high school football recruit for 2006, ahead of Matthew Stafford and Tim Tebow. Rivals.com named me the most athletic recruit in the nation. I received eighty-three scholarship offers from Division One programs.

Today, I don't speak to many people from my prep school days, other than Bridgette. Yet people from my class love to write on my Instagram. *I went to school with him! Great football player and the nicest kid.* Those comments mean nothing to me, summon no pangs of nostalgia. Sometimes I hear my friends reminisce about warm memories of their high school days: freestyle rapping in the back of the buses, playing hooky on senior skip day, or going to Disney World. I can't relate. I traded the comfort of good times with people of my own persuasion for my education. Unfortunately, that education included a master class in white privilege.

● ● ●

Once I was named the top prospect in the nation, I didn't have the bandwidth for much of a social life, even if I had wanted one. Recruiting and media attention ate up all my free time. My flip phone rang with calls from the *New York Times*, *USA Today*, *Sports Illustrated for Kids*, and ESPN. Reporters loved me because I gave them good sound bites; I could put together cogent sentences that read well in print. My story wasn't what they usually covered: the number one player in the country from a boarding school that looks like something out of *A Separate Peace*. Kids that hit people as hard as I did typically didn't play for New Jersey prep schools.

I even did a photo shoot for a magazine where they put me in a Sean John suit. In the spread, I'm sitting with my legs crossed and a football in my hand. I looked clean. I was hoping to keep the gear, but it would have been an NCAA recruiting violation.

I was able to withstand the pressure of this attention because Cory was a buffer, my agent before I had an agent. When recruiters would call him, he'd filter out the noise, passing along only the necessary information. He was all business. "Myron, Miami wants to talk to you. Ohio State wants to talk to you."

"I got thirty minutes. Let's talk."

When I was busy at practice or sitting around a Harkness table, Cory gave quotes to magazines on my behalf. He knew exactly what to say to make me sound like the young man I was on my way to becoming. Cory's shouldering part of my load allowed me to focus on my studies, my training, and making the small adjustments needed to stay on top of the rankings.

Top college coaches read those articles. Soon they flocked to Hun's campus. Urban Meyer from Florida, Pete Carroll from USC, Jim Tressel from Ohio State, Bobby Bowden of Florida State, Joe Paterno from Penn State, and Charlie Weis from Notre Dame—they all showed up at Hun's gate.

I remember the day Charlie Weis came to visit. A sports figure of that stature had never come to Hun before, and the campus was buzzing. All my coaches were acting like fanboys in Weis's presence as we sat down together at an old posh table in a meeting room away from prying eyes. An NCAA recruiting rule states that a coach cannot speak directly to a player, so Charlie sat across the table from me, and my head coach acted as an intermediary.

"I want you to tell Myron that we want him at Notre Dame, and if he comes to Notre Dame, he can get one of these," Weis told my coach. He pulled out his New England Patriots Super Bowl ring and handed it to my coach, who placed it in my palm. I slipped it on with shaking hands. It was heavy—not only physically heavy, although the diamonds glittering in it weren't small, but also emotionally heavy. It represented the final goal of every young person who plays football.

The recruiting pitches kept pouring in. Most football programs did their homework and didn't approach me with money, cars, or girls. They knew that would be a surefire way to have Cory hang up the phone—something he did more than once. The smart schools appealed to my surgical ambitions, which I had mentioned to ESPN. "You can get your doctorate at our school," they told me. "You can shadow doctors as an undergrad." When I went on recruiting trips, I was able to meet the deans of medical schools and neurosurgeons teaching at PhD programs. Universities trotted out their presidents, who introduced me to Rhodes and Fulbright Scholars. I took dozens of tours of university hospitals and medical science buildings.

The big guns really pulled out all the stops. USC brought me down to the field of the Coliseum and had their Song Girls dance around me. "Myron! How are you?" a dozen pretty voices chimed. "How's the Hun School this year? The East Coast must be so cold." I wondered how they knew where I went to high school—I'd never met them before in my life. One Song Girl grabbed my arm and said, laughing, "I've been to the Bahamas before. I loved the water. So blue!"

"How do you know I'm from the islands?" I asked, my head swimming. Instead of answering, she flashed an ultrabeaming smile at me and shook her pom-poms. I learned later that the coaches had written out a report on me that they had the Song Girls review before my campus visit.

All this attention was intoxicating, but my family reminded me to be about my business. I knew what these schools were doing. I loved it, and it felt good, but at the end of the day, I needed to find the right school that would prepare me for everything I wanted to achieve. I couldn't let the Hollywood glamour distract me. If I let that noise in, I would have been signed with USC in a second. I had to think deeper than just the thrill and excitement of being a football player in a glamorous town.

The moment I stepped on Florida State University's campus,

I found the balance I had been looking for. That's not to say the Seminoles were opposed to a little pomp and circumstance. When the recruiter was showing me around the football offices, he paused in front of a closed door and flashed me a devious smile. "Myron, are you ready for this?" he asked.

"Ready for what?"

He threw open the door to reveal a room filled with faces I recognized. FSU quarterback legend Chris Rix, running back Lorenzo Booker, head coach Bobby Bowden, university president T. K. Wetherell, and dozens of other football personas cheered my entrance as though I had walked into a surprise birthday party. Somebody cued the music, and the Big Tymers track "Get Your Roll On" blasted through the room. "Everybody, get your roll on. Everybody, everybody, get your roll on," the crowd chanted, jumping up and down.

"That's so tough, that's so tough," I shouted while shaking what seemed like a hundred hands.

Later that night, I had dinner with T. K. Wetherell and Coach Bowden. President Wetherell's head was bandaged; he explained that earlier in the day he had fallen while jogging in Doak Campbell Stadium, suffering lacerations and a concussion. Doctors at Tallahassee Memorial Hospital advised that he needed to stay under their supervision overnight. He rebuffed them, saying, "I need to be out of here in an hour or two. The number one recruit in the nation is visiting Florida State, and I have to be there to help the football team get this kid." He took a couple of painkillers and made it back to FSU to meet me.

"This is a tough guy," I thought. "If he is emblematic of what FSU is about, then this might be the place for me."

As our plates were cleared away, T. K. said casually, "Look who just texted me."

He handed me his flip phone. On the screen was a message from Governor Jeb Bush. "Myron, welcome to Florida State," it said. "You are the model student athlete. I hope you choose FSU."

After dinner Coach Bowden took me up to his office. Bowden could speak to me directly because I was visiting *his* campus, while coaches like Charlie Weis had to communicate in code because they were visiting *my* high school. It's one of those quirky NCAA rules.

Bowden had a huge, well-worn Bible on his desk. "What's your favorite verse, Myron?"

"Hebrews 13:6."

"Recite it for me, if you don't mind."

"The Lord is my helper. I shall not fear what man shall do unto me."

"I'm glad you chose that verse, son."

We started going through Scripture together, talking about the importance of my being a better man, being a better citizen, and being a better husband in the future. He didn't talk about being an All-Pro or an All-American or a Heisman Trophy winner. He told me, "When I finish this life, I want my players and I want you, Myron, to have known Christ and to join me in heaven. If I can do that, then I've won. That's more important than any championship." FSU's football coach and leader—the best football coach in the country, maybe one of the best football coaches of all time—was speaking to me about my faith and growing as a Christian man, not about beating the University of Miami.

FSU spoke to the chip on my shoulder, spoke to the *dog* I had in me, and spoke to the toughness that I wanted to exemplify. On top of that, Tallahassee, Florida, is a predominantly Black city, and players on the team were pretty much all Black. After four years in a sea of unseasoned chicken and potato salad with raisins, I wanted a culture shift. The icing on the cake was when they told me that an illustrious alum, Garrett Johnson, would be my mentor if I chose to attend. Garrett had won a Rhodes Scholarship at FSU while competing as a shot-putter, and they assured me I could do the same. FSU had every base covered. They believed in me as a Christian man of faith. They also saw me as a future Rhodes Scholar foremost and as a football player second. I made my choice, and Daddy gave me his stamp of approval.

When I got back to Hun, I had the idea of lining up all the hats representing the college finalists on a table in front of me— Miami, Texas, Penn State, Florida, and Oklahoma—and declaring my choice on live TV. ESPN agreed to do the broadcast, but when they tried to work out the logistics, school officials decided they did not want a camera crew on campus. Never mind that the QB from the previous year had a camera crew broadcast his decision— and never mind that this player's father had just donated money to build a new game field for the team. When I suggested I make the announcement with my teammates in Atlantic City, school officials objected to this, too, because they didn't want their students to be in an environment of gambling and alcohol.

I have to ask: Was the image of a proud young Black man asserting his future the problem? It would not be the last time I would have to ask this question of institutional powers. Though the slight stung, my brother Whitney's words echoed in my ears. *Do not let those who wish you failure be albatrosses to your ascension.*

Chapter 3

HIT SOMEBODY

My senior year at Hun, I marveled watching Big Ten Freshman of the Year Maurice Clarett drive his shoulder through armies of linebackers as he racked up 1,237 yards to set the freshman rushing record at Ohio State. In the second overtime of the 2002 National Championship, announcer Keith Jackson's operatic voice called out, "Clarett! Touchdown!" Clarett and the Buckeyes capped a perfect 14–0 record by raising that glittering crystal trophy.

I wanted to have that kind of impact right away at Florida State. Clarett had graduated high school early to get a jump on the college game. I decided to mirror his approach, churning through my coursework at Hun as fast as New Jersey state law would allow. By January 2016, I had my nose stuck in a two-hundred-page playbook in a team suite in Tallahassee, Florida. Most of the other incoming freshmen wouldn't arrive until spring training. I gave myself four extra months to learn 150 defense packages, hone my body with winter conditioning, and earn a place in the starting lineup.

I lived with three upperclassmen: our starting offensive lineman, our backup linebacker, and one of our starting receivers, Southern boys from Florida and Georgia. I walked in wearing a fit influenced by Jay-Z to a house full of guys with braids bumping Trick

Daddy and Rick Ross while they cooked up country-fried steak. They drank gallons of sweet tea, which tasted like someone had dumped sugar into battery acid.

These guys came from a different world. Many of them had grown up eating mayonnaise sandwiches in public housing. Some of their slang and, more critically, the life experience that vernacular grew out of was lost in translation. One night our receiver asked me, "Hey, man, you got a jit?"

What's a jit? I asked myself. *I suppose jit sounds like dancing?* "No, I don't have a dance tonight," I replied.

The whole room busted up. "Nah, man, nah," my teammates said. "Do you got a kid, a jitterbug, a little kid?"

"Oh, nah," I said.

"Myron wouldn't have a jit," our lineman said. "He's too deep in the books for women."

I'd shown my suitemates my schedule to see if we'd have any courses together. I was already a sophomore in standing but figured since they were older, we might overlap. They looked at the list of honors courses and medical school electives and said, "Man, that's a part of campus we've never even seen before."

The feeling of disconnect was familiar, just calibrated differently. I worked out with these guys throughout winter conditioning, but I was working *alongside* them, not *with* them. They made it clear that simply putting on the garnet and gold didn't make me part of the family.

In early practices, I was the recipient of more than a few late hits from Buster Davis, a linebacker who grew up in Daytona, Florida. He nicknamed himself "the Mouth of the South." That suited Buster: a big, big talker and a small, small linebacker. His mouth was larger than his body.

"I don't respect players who aren't from Florida," he told me, right up in my face. "You don't play the kind of football we play down here."

I would hear Buster telling the other guys that I wasn't worthy of being a Seminole. Prep school made me soft. Too much hype. That made me want to play a hundred times as hard as he did. I decided that whenever the whistle blew to stop play, the echo in my ears would be from me always being the last one to crack a hit.

I was grateful for the extra time I had given myself. These were grown men with grown bodies. They moved as fast as I did, and they were bigger than me. Everyone was a five-star athlete who walked with confidence and assurance. Their goal, like mine, was a National Championship and the NFL. From the first workouts, an unrelenting competition level set a high threshold I would have to cross to become a Seminole.

Being a Seminole meant being a part of the storied tradition of Florida State football. The legacy is long and well documented: three national championships, eighteen conference titles and six division titles, three undefeated seasons, forty-one straight winning seasons from 1977 through 2017, and three Heisman Trophy winners: quarterbacks Charlie Ward in 1993, Chris Weinke in 2000, and Jameis Winston in 2013. Scores of players have gone to the NFL, many becoming stars.

Since I'd never really connected with my high school peers, I wanted to be a part of the family that would continue this history. I saw a couple of avenues on how to become a Seminole. One would be through my play—being so impressive that I would force myself into the conversation. The second would be trying to integrate into FSU football culture, fitting in with the team. My teammates liked to play *Madden* and spades, and we didn't listen to the same sorts of music. I tried to hang, but I didn't come to college to sit and smoke weed in a starter's entourage. I had calculus class. My course load earned me the nickname "Smart Boy," a moniker I was determined to change.

I found commonality with Lorenzo Booker, a senior getting ready to enter the next NFL draft. I'd first come across him in the pages of *ESPN* magazine, marveling when this California football phenom spoke of the importance of academics. Lorenzo embraced me not because I was a great player but because we had similar stories. The number one player in high school, and the most sought after running back in five years, Lorenzo had announced his college decision on national TV after receiving sixty scholarships. We both came from out of state, so a lot of eyes were on us. He knew what it was like to have ESPN shadow you for weeks.

Lorenzo cast his own formidable shadow on FSU. When you ball as beautifully as Lorenzo did, the world opens up to you. One day I was sitting on my couch, reading an organic chemistry textbook, when my phone rang.

"What are you doing?"

I looked down at the page: *reactions and preparation of carbon-containing compounds, which include not only hydrocarbons but also compounds with any number of other elements, including hydrogen (most compounds contain at least one carbon-hydrogen bond), nitrogen.* "Chilling, man," I said. "I'm just watching SportsCenter."

"I'll be outside in ten minutes. Put some clothes on. We're going to the club."

"What are you talking about?"

"Ten minutes."

The line went dead. I scrambled to shower and put on some clothes. I'd never been to a North Florida club and had no idea what to wear. Precisely ten minutes later, Lorenzo's tires screeched outside. I went out to see him in a fresh silver sedan with three women in the back. Lorenzo didn't have a car of his own—he would always roll up in the car of whatever woman he was hanging with. One day it might be a red sports car, another day it would be a Range Rover, the next it might be a Hummer.

"Girls," Lorenzo said. "Say hi to Myron."

"Hi, Myron!"

I didn't know what Lorenzo was talking about when he said "girls." These were fully grown *women*, with grown features, and they weren't wearing capris with sweaters tied around their waists like the girls at Hun. And they were saying hi to me as if I were someone important.

I waved back as I got in the car, but the protective shell around my psyche that had calcified at Hun thought, "I don't know who any of you are, and I don't know where we're going."

Lorenzo didn't share my shyness. When we walked into the club, the DJ cut the Flo Rida song and boomed over the sound system, "Lorenzo. Booker. Is. In. The. House."

"Yeah, and he's with Myron Rolle, the next coming," Lorenzo shouted back.

"The next coming Myron Rolleeeee," the DJ called, dropping Yung Joc's "It's Goin' Down."

Lorenzo was the don: whenever the masses of characters that orbited Florida State football came up to shake Lorenzo's hand, he'd say, "You got to meet my boy Myron Rolle." A sea of interchangeable faces appeared before my eyes, rotating like the numbers in a slot machine. I knew nothing would come of most of these handshakes, and that was fine by me.

The girls we had come with could see that I was a bit awkward in this setting, so they tried to be good sports. "What's going on?" they asked me over the thud of the bass.

"I'm good. I'm straight." I was parroting phrases from music videos. What was I doing in the club? I had just finished reading about catalysts and enzymatic activity.

The girls knew I was green, and they could sense that I was likely to stay that way. I didn't drink, and I could count on one hand the number of times I'd been to the club.

Clubs like these were the operating zones for street agents, underhand dealers that worked off the books for big sports agents who wanted to represent you in the NFL. They'd try to slip into your inner circles, buy you drinks and tables, to butter you up to sign with their boss when you hit the league. That night a street agent came up and said, "I work for ———. I just want to let you know, anything you need, bro, anything you need. He's got you, I've got you."

These extracurriculars never held much mystique. They carried too high a risk.

Thankfully, my reputation as a model student-athlete shielded me from most of the street agents. If being smart protected me from the seedy side of football, that was one more incentive to play up that part of my image.

Lorenzo drove me home that night. I was grateful he had taken me under his wing, but I wouldn't be hitting the club again soon. Lorenzo had earned a few nights out on the town; I still hadn't connected with my teammates or earned my spot in the starting rotation. Every moment spent at the club could have been used to study coverage. I needed to focus on building relationships, studying for my premed track, and, frankly, balling.

Because balling was what I was at Florida State to do. And the man I had to impress was Mickey Andrews. Florida State's defensive coordinator was a six-foot-one gentleman from Ozark, Alabama, with salt-and-pepper hair peeking out from under a garnet FSU hat. He wore dark glasses even when we practiced into the evenings, and you could tell his broad shoulders and big calves had supported a muscular build back in the day. He played wide receiver and defensive back at the University of Alabama for the legendary Paul "Bear" Bryant, earning his spot in the Alabama Sports Hall of Fame.

Coach Andrews still walked like the athlete he had once been. He moved with a smoothness that said, *There's power in my presence.* He would spit when he yelled, he would spit when he cussed, and he did a lot of both. If I fouled up one of his carefully drawn plays, he would say in his gruff way, "Myron, you're the dumbest-a—smart kid I've ever met in my life." If I let a wide-out slip by me into the end zone, I would earn a, "Myron, I bet if that receiver were an organic chemistry test, you would have destroyed him." He'd find your button, and then he'd slam his finger on it.

One day in spring training, a corner from Delaware named Ed Imeokparia couldn't cover the slant route. Ed got beat, over and over and over again. Coach Andrews blew the whistle and walked to the middle of the field, talking loud enough that the whole team could hear. "Ed, if I can go to my savings account, move some money over," he mused while looking up in the sky, squinting with concentration. "Move some money over to the checking, and if I got enough. I'll have to check with my wife, but if I have enough money . . ."

All the freshmen looked at each other, confused.

"If I can do that," he said, "I think I might have enough d— money to get you a Greyhound bus ticket and send your a— back to Delaware."

The setup for that slam took almost a full minute, and poor Ed had to stand in the middle of the field and take it.

But after practice, when you walked off the field after giving everything you had, Coach Andrews would put his arm around you, kiss you, and tell you he loved you. "You know, Myron, I love you. You know that, right?"

"You love me? You just killed me out there, telling me that I was interested more in organic chemistry than—"

"I had to say that, Myron. You know I love you. You know."

Coach Andrews showed that love by teaching our team about the 2% Way. He helped us see that daily, minor improvements are a tangible way to realize our full potential. Not only that, but he also told us it could become helpful groundwork for our lives: if you adopt the 2 percent approach, you'll find that every day is positive and every day is a movement forward. As I've noted, this idea would end up shaping the rest of my life.

Before I adopted this approach, achievement carried a pressure that could morph into stress. I felt the burden of getting as much done as quickly as possible. After I adopted the 2 percent mentality, I learned that life is not about making giant leaps—or paying back the debt you felt you owed in one lump sum. If you obsess over big paybacks, you put too much pressure on yourself, and you end up making wrong short-term decisions. Over time, small improvements will lead to huge gains, but it happens a little bit at a time.

Coach Andrews used the 2% Way to make sure I understood what I needed to become a starter at FSU. He would yell at practice, "Myron, two percent better on your backpedal, two percent!" And so it would sort of lock into your mind, "I need to focus on my backpedal, making sure that my hips are low and my knees are bent, my arms are swinging. I need to drive out of my break so that I can make the play on this wide receiver." I saw on film that I was a little bit too high. My break wasn't fast enough or sharp enough. Instead of beating me down, Coach's 2% Way built me up every day. If I could get two percent lower on my backpedal each day, I'd be ten percent better by the end of the week. Two percent was an attainable goal, something I could strive for at every practice.

Coach Andrews made me focus on the deficit of my game by yelling out, "Two percent, Myron, two percent!" Whenever there was a weak spot in my game, Coach would yell, "Two percent higher, Myron. Two percent sooner, Myron."

The 2% Way became hardwired into my psyche. Each day when I left the field, Coach would ask me if I'd gotten 2 percent better. It made me feel good about the practice that day. I felt like I had moved 2 percent closer to the player I wanted to be, two percent closer to becoming a starter at Florida State, 2 percent closer to playing on Sundays: the NFL.

Florida is hot in the summer. I don't mean New Jersey hot. I mean Florida hot: 100-degree heat with 100-percent humidity. There were times I thought I was going to die on that football field. "I'm done," I thought as sweat ran into my eyes so heavily I couldn't see. In my head, I started talking to saints and my ancestors who were already in heaven. "I'm going to meet the good Lord right now. Saint Thomas, Saint Paul, I'm about to see y'all. Mary Magdalene, what's up? Set aside a table for me because I'm about to meet y'all right now. Granddaddy, I'm coming home."

Just when I thought my tank was empty and I couldn't give any more, Coach Andrews would say, "You got this, Myron. You can give me more. Give me two percent more of who you are. Show me two percent more of what you can do."

Coach Andrews believed in me. He showed me the way to give two percent more than I thought was possible. For some reason, because Coach believed it, I believed it. I knew he had coached with legendary Alabama coach Bear Bryant. He had been there with the man who was synonymous with excellence. He had coached men into the NFL.

That's when I really started believing in myself. I'd always had confidence, but this was different, deeper. "Man, Coach was right. I did have more in me than I thought I had." Coach encouraged and motivated me to improve every play, every day.

Our team's collective buy-in to the 2% Way was how I finally connected with my teammates. After Coach Andrews had wrung all he could out of us, we would sit in the locker room, soaked in sweat in a way only summer football practice can produce, unable to move. I caught knowing smiles, as if my teammates were saying, "Boy, we made it through that together." We knew practice had been ruthless when Kirk Franklin would start to play in the locker room. Only gospel music can heal the pain of sixty punishment wind sprints because a corner dropped a pick-six. "It's over now, and I feel like I can make it. The storm is over now," came Franklin's tenor, and then, softly, the lineman began to groan the lyrics. A linebacker, knees in ice, joined in. "It's over now. It's over now." I added my voice to the chorus, too exhausted to care if others thought I belonged.

That small inroad through music gave me an idea. If practice wasn't devilish enough to require gospel, a big group of players would throw on a Rick Ross beat in the locker room and spit some real slow Southern raps over the thudding bass. If I could learn to freestyle and do it well, my teammates might look at me as something other than Smart Boy.

I took this new skill very seriously. Besides football, it might have been one of the first tasks I tackled with the 2% Way. I searched YouTube for popular freestyle beats and spent the few spare minutes I had putting together rhymes. Luckily, quite a few words rhyme with Rolle. Once I had something I knew wasn't complete trash, I tried to make it two percent better by adding some twist to it, some wordplay I knew the guys would rock with.

I improved that rough draft by accounting for freestyling's spontaneity, anticipating what outfits the guys would be wearing and filing away their football miscues and bloopers in a mental Rolodex. I added those elements to my lyrics. Soon I had nine or ten raps ready for whatever scenario might occur.

The next time they put on a Trick Daddy beat I had studied up on, I joined the circle. Preston Parker, now a professional rapper, finished up his verse, and our running back Antone Smith hopped on the track. Antone came from Pahokee, Florida, and spit his bars through a mouth full of permanent gold teeth.

When Antone paused, I jumped in. The stakes were high: a wack rap would follow me like a nasty rumor. "M dot Rolle, I rock number three, from a small state they call Jersey." I saw Antone look at Preston Parker: *Okay, let's give Smart Boy a chance.* I started going in, combining my prepared material with what had happened at practice that morning. "Jookin in The Moon where all my peeps be, in the VIP so you can't peep me." The Moon was the hottest club in Tallahassee, the spot where T-Pain hung out. Guys started shouting, shocked that the nerd could stay on the beat and beat it up. They didn't know about the hours of work I had put in. I had prepared for the fact that it had to seem unprepared—calculated spontaneity.

Antone and Preston were impressed. The door into their world had opened just a crack for Smart Boy.

But it wasn't smooth sailing. Buster Davis, the Mouth of the South, never stopped yapping at me. One day during the summer, when Daddy had come down to Tallahassee to watch practice, the Mouth came at me harder than usual. Daddy had a chair by the sidelines, and I sat down in it during a water break. I didn't see any reason why it should go unused. Buster had other ideas.

"You better get the f—— up out of that chair," he snapped.

I hated when people cussed in front of my father. At home, I would have caught hands for that kind of language. I didn't hold my tongue. "Why are you paying me so much attention, number one?" I shot back.

"Get the f—— up right now."

I pointed to the other players sitting on benches and coolers. "We got eighty guys on the field, but you're looking at me."

Daddy, worried about the ramifications of my taking on a team captain, said gently, "Myron, just get up."

I turned to him. "Hold on, Daddy. This isn't right."

"Myron, for now, just get up." Daddy was always thinking about the road ahead, how to flip a bad situation into a positive one.

I took a deep breath and stood. Buster got deeper into my space. "We don't sit in no f—— chair, man."

"Buster, chill out. And stop cussing in front of my father."

"F—— no, I ain't f—— chilling out."

"Okay," I said. "I got something for you."

"Oh, now Smart Boy upset. Hey!" Buster yelled out to the team. "Smart Boy is mad now."

I don't know if it was the chip on my shoulder or the frank disrespect of having somebody call me out and cuss at me in front of my family, but I was fired up. If he couldn't shut his mouth, I was going to close it for him. I was going to introduce a little East Coast manners to the Mouth of the South.

But this wasn't high school. Fighting a team captain of a Division One football program would have serious consequences. So before I went Pompey on him, I talked to Coach Andrews. "Coach," I said, "I'm about to put my hands on your captain." I said, "I just want to make sure that if I do this, that you're not going to suspend me."

"Just ignore Buster. Play your game. You're great," Coach told me. He was right. I didn't want to have the reputation of being a player who couldn't hold his water and had a temper. Resorting to violence would hurt me in the eyes of my teammates, my coaches, and the NFL. So I laid off Buster. He kept talking, but I never said anything back to him. I vowed to let my play close his mouth for good.

• • •

The summer before the fall season of 2006 was brutally hot and muggy. There wasn't a breeze to be found in Tallahassee. The heat sat on us. We were running 110-yard sprints, and I felt as if a wet towel had been jammed down my throat. When you get to the twentieth 110-yard sprint, you just want the torture to cease.

Our strength coach, Coach Stroud, let us box our way out of sprints. Defensive player versus offensive player. Whoever won, that side of the ball didn't have to run. On went headgear, eight-pound gloves, and mouthpieces. We stood in a circle, and the two gladiators would wail on each other. I mean, guys went *after* it. We didn't know how to box; we were just throwing bombs.

The first couple of bouts heavily favored the offense. They worked through our defense pretty quickly. I knew my number was due to be called. Many nights that summer, I went home and looked up highlights of Sugar Ray Leonard, Muhammad Ali, and Roy Jones Jr. I shadowboxed in my room, trying to make each jab two percent faster, two percent more accurate, two percent more punishing. I watched the films over and over again, moving my head, bobbing, weaving, jabbing. I practiced putting together combinations. Jab,

jab, left hook, right hook. When they called my name, I would be ready. I would stand up, and I would deliver.

The next day we were sprinting our fifteenth 110-yarder when Coach Stroud blew the whistle, shouting, "Okay, all right, we can stop it right now and box it out." The coach called out a name: "Marcus Simms." Marcus Simms was a linebacker turned fullback. He was 240 pounds of solid muscle who played with the speed of a running back and the anger of a linebacker. "Marcus Simms, who are you going to box?"

Marcus called out, "I want three." That was my number. When he said, "I want three," that was the moment I had the chance to truly become a Florida State Seminole and be a *part* of the team, not just *on* the team.

I popped up, literally springing to my feet. "I've been waiting on you, Marcus," I thought, as the defense chanted: "All right, all right. Let's go, three. Let's go, three." I put on a headpiece, taped up my gloves, and bit down on the mouth guard.

The boys got in the circle, and Coach Stroud shouted, "Let's go, fight." I started out like Sugar Ray Leonard, all sweetness and guile. Jab, jab, move, jab, move, stick, move, hook, move, stick, move, jab, move. I'm six foot two, 218 pounds. Marcus was maybe five foot eleven, 240 pounds. I knew if he got too close, he'd have the edge on me. But I'm longer, faster, and quicker. I used my reach to my advantage and stayed away from his power. He tried an uppercut. It missed. I stayed outside, using my length to land punches outside his reach. I worked the body and the head, always moving in and out. He couldn't get a clean knockout shot in. I systematically broke him down. I took him apart piece by piece with surgical precision.

The whistle blew, signaling the end of round one. By now, the defense was firmly in my corner, "Yo, let's go, Rolle. Let's go." They were fired up. They had no idea that I could dish it out like that, just as they didn't have any idea that I could freestyle. I stood up and went back into the circle with the confidence of Muhammad Ali.

Boom, boom, stick, move, stick, jab, jab, move, hook, move, stick, move. Simms threw a haymaker. I dodged it. The missed punch made him stumble, and he nearly fell to the ground. Simms was being embarrassed; he couldn't lay a glove on me.

When the second round ended, the defense shouted, "And the winner is . . . we ain't even gotta say it." My boys lifted me onto their shoulders and chanted, "Let's go, Rolle. Let's go."

Back in the locker room, players patted me on the back. "Man, I didn't know you had that in you, three."

"Man, three, man, I'm impressed."

"You were amazing, bro."

"That was great, man. That was great."

That was one of the best days of my college experience. As I was walking off the field, I remember an offensive player sidled up to me. "Hey, three," he said. "I'll be honest with you, bro. I thought you were soft before today. But, bro, you want to hang later?"

All I could think was, "That's all it took? Now I can come over and hang with you dudes? I don't smoke weed. I don't drink. I don't play video games. I'm not great at spades. I don't do any of the things that you like to do. I don't listen to your music, but now you want me to come because I beat up one of the Florida boys." I had finally earned their respect.

Word got to Coach Andrews. He called me up and said, "Myron, I just heard you whooped Marcus Simms's a—."

All I said was, "Yes, Coach." I'd already done my talking in the ring.

"You've got guts."

• • •

From that day on, my name changed from "Smart Boy" or "Three" to "President Rolle" or "Doctor Rolle." My teammates included me in more of their activities. We went to the barbershop together. We took road trips to Atlanta. We started watching the *Fresh Prince of Bel-Air* and *Martin* on DVD together.

Best of all, the guys would include me in their conversation and look at me as an intellectual they respected. "Hey, President, come over here." And they would ask me, "Hey, President, is Tunisia a country in North Africa, or is that in the Caribbean?"

"It's in North Africa."

"Man, Dr. Rolle said it, man. He said it. It's over. It's done. Don't need no Google." I became the Alex Trebek of the team.

The sense of belonging let me focus on football. My confidence soared, and I began to play better. I was born to be a safety: the last line of defense. Safeties position themselves the farthest from the line of scrimmage, the imaginary line that separates the offense and defense. And there are typically three layers of the defense. There's the defensive line, big, stout, stocky guys who fight in the trenches. Behind them are the linebackers, smaller but faster and more violent. They stalk the middle area of the field between the linemen and the defensive backs.

It was my job to survey everything that's happening on the field in front of me. From my vantage point, I could see everything. I could see the receivers lined up wide. I could see the quarterback, all the linemen. I could call out coverages to the guys in front of me. "Strong left" or "Strong right." "Watch the go route on eighty."

Seeing what no one else could see was an integral part of my role. I liked seeing the whole picture and making snap decisions. Communication made me a leader.

I balled out all spring and summer in preparation for the fall football season. *Sporting News* heralded me as the second coming of Deion Sanders, who starred at Florida State before he played for the Dallas Cowboys. When *NCAA Football* came out on PlayStation, I was rated as one of my team's best players, a 93 out of 100. The only FSU player who was rated higher than me was my friend Lorenzo Booker. He was a 98.

The PlayStation game had made me a starter. It was *the* talk of the locker room. People were looking at the ratings and feeling disrespected.

"D—, Rolle, they got you running. Your speed is ninety-eight. I'm faster than you."

"You start now, Doctor Rolle? That's news to me."

The truth was, I wasn't yet a starter. Coach Andrews didn't want to put me on the field before I was ready, sending me to the wolves in the first game of the season against our rival, the University of Miami. The game was on national TV.

Coach Andrews was protective, but I was eighteen years old, supremely confident in my ability and ready to start. The lights weren't too bright for me. I wanted to shine in front of a national television audience of millions. Everyone I knew in the Bahamas would be sitting in front of a television watching me.

I played a total of six snaps.

Apparently, the coaches had not seen the PlayStation ratings. I watched from the sidelines as the lights shone on others. My friends back home in the Bahamas called me up and gave it to me. "Hey, bey, look here. I was watching the game, and I didn't see you play one snap, mon."

After a few more games of biding my time on the sidelines, my attitude shifted. I didn't feel motivated to get 2 percent better every day if I wasn't going to be on the field. After one practice where I missed a few assignments, Kevin Steele, the linebackers coach, called me into his office. "I don't see the same passion that you had when you first came in," he told me. "That bright-eyed, bushy-tailed, young freshman that you were."

"Coach, you guys are trying my patience right now," I said. "You know I should be starting at safety. I make good plays when I'm on the field. I don't know what's going on."

"Myron, we know you're a better player than the guy we have out there," the coach said. "We know you're more talented than him. We get it. We can all see it. We've been coaching football longer than you've been alive, so you got to trust us on this. We want you to dominate from the second you step on that field. We want to make sure that you're in a position to do that."

"I'm ready now."

"Let me tell you a story about a safety named Mike Minter," he said. "When I was coaching for Nebraska, he was a superstar freshman like you. He thought he should be starting as well. He was plenty good, but we didn't start him until the ninth game of his freshman year. He was upset, but when he went onto that field, he dominated. He became an All-American and then played ten years with the Carolina Panthers as a safety. He became an All-Pro. He had a great career. You're better than Mike Minter, and you can have a career like him."

My spirits lifted. If they had done it before with a guy like Mike Minter, then maybe I could still have those opportunities too. I would be patient a little longer. Two days later, the starter went down with a knee injury. It was my turn now. I balled out against Rice. I had nine tackles, a pass breakup, and a fumble recovery. I played like a man possessed. I never left the field again. The rest of the freshman season happened just as Coach said it would. I ended up being a freshman All-American and All-ACC.

The team went 6–6 my freshman year and earned a spot against UCLA in the Emerald Bowl at AT&T Park in San Francisco. Traveling always makes me hungry, and after we got into town, I had a hankering for some late-night breakfast. It was late December, only a few days before Christmas, and the restaurants lining the block near the team hotel had locked their doors. My phone informed me that a Denny's was six blocks away. I marched into the unfamiliar city in search of French toast.

As I walked, the streets emptied, drab concrete and drawn metal gates replacing San Francisco's bustle. A few cab drivers shared a cigarette under a glowing, yellow Denny's sign. Both of the *n*'s had burned out. I felt pangs of hunger and loneliness as I pushed open the door and took a seat alone.

A faint, artificial light coated the diner's chipped tabletops and the few patrons' drawn faces. It was the kind of place that made you want to call your mother. I realized that my waitress, who approached my table in a gray T-shirt stained with egg yolk, was older than my mother. She looked nearly seventy. I could tell she had been on her feet for hours, yet she smiled at me when I ordered a Lumberjack Slam.

In her smile, I saw a life of struggle and disappointment. In the wrinkles of the skin below her eyes, there lived a pain that I felt viscerally. It was in the way she carried the menus; it was how she pronounced each word slowly to mask her thick accent. Without warning, that pain reached out and touched a part of me I didn't know existed. And I felt it. I felt it more acutely than I had ever felt anything. I did not know this woman's name. I hadn't spoken to her except to order pancakes and sausage. Yet I could sense without a doubt that she'd had a tough go of it. I wasn't sure if she was an immigrant who had escaped some dire conflict; I wasn't sure if she had a family that she didn't see. I only knew she was hurting on the night shift in a Denny's in a hard part of town.

Within seconds, I was hurting too. The connectivity between us dropped her pain directly into my soul, and I was moved to the point of breaking down. Even now, as I recount this, I can still recall a piece of that ripping feeling in my soul. I shook as I choked down my eggs and put down all the money in my wallet for a tip.

As soon as I went outside, I started crying. Crying isn't something I do much of, but I was sobbing so hard I could barely see the street in front of me. The cab drivers, who were still smoking, probably thought I was nuts. I pulled out my cell phone and called Coach Andrews. He picked up on the first ring.

"Coach, are you at the hotel?"

"Yeah, Myron, I'm here."

"I need to talk to you right away."

"Are you okay?"

"Coach, I have to talk to you."

"Room 1207."

"I'm on my way."

College coaches are used to getting calls like this late at night. All sorts of trouble can go down leading up to a bowl game. But I don't think Coach Andrews thought it would be me on the other end of the line.

I tried to calm myself on the walk back to the hotel. Inside Coach Andrews's room, I sat on the couch, and he sat across from me in a chair. "Myron, is everything all right?" he asked. His voice was concerned but not angry.

I let it go, ugly crying, uncontrollable tears and snot streaming out in equal measure. I tried to speak, hyperventilating between half-formed words. "This woman . . . I . . . know her . . . I felt . . . her."

"Slow down, slow down. Tell me what happened."

I managed to steady my breath enough to form sentences and told Coach Andrews in detail. "It's hard to describe," I told him. "It was like she reached out and touched me. Her hand was burning hot." I needed to make sense of what had happened, why I felt the searing pain of another in my spirit. I needed to know why I didn't care that I was bawling in front of my rough, gruff coach in his room at ten at night when we were scheduled to play a bowl game in four days.

Coach Andrews looked relieved. "Myron, that was the Lord working through you. He wanted you to reach out to that woman. Find out her story, pray for her, touch her."

"How come it felt like I was being torn apart?"

"It's a powerful feeling, especially if it's the first time that has happened to you. You were confused, and you were alone in a strange city. But I guarantee you when that happens again, and if you talk to that person, they won't be a stranger to you anymore. God doesn't want that person to be a stranger to you. You never know what beauty comes from that."

Understanding and clarity flooded into me. We prayed together, and when I got up to leave, Coach Andrews hugged me.

As soon as I was back to my room, the phone rang. "Myron, I was in the bathroom while you were talking to Mickey, and I heard everything, son," Coach Andrews's wife Diane's voice twanged. Like her husband, she's from Ozark, Alabama.

"That's okay, it's your room," I said.

"I just wanted to tell you, I'm praying for you. We love you so much. It took courage for you to come in here."

I appreciated her kindness. She didn't have to call me, but she knew I was hurting. "I have an idea, Myron," she continued. "Would you be willing to do something?"

"What's that?" I asked.

"After dinner tomorrow, you, me, and Mickey are all going to get dressed up, and we're going to take a taxi to talk to that woman. We're going to pray for her, and we're going to bless her. How does that sound?"

That sounded like exactly the balm my soul needed. The next night, Christmas Eve, I put on a nice suit and met Coach and Mrs. Andrews in the lobby. They were dressed to the nines. We stepped outside and approached a taxi driver idling outside his cab.

"You going to a Christmas party?" the cab driver asked.

"Take us to Denny's," I replied.

When we pulled up, the yellow Denny's sign was dark, the doors locked. We had forgotten that even Denny's closes on Christmas Eve.

"It's a blessing," Coach Andrews said.

"How's that?" I asked.

"She's not working on Christmas."

I didn't get to talk to that woman, and I never met her again. But I feel her spirit to this day.

In the Emerald Bowl, I had my first career interception and nine tackles.

When I returned from winter break, Coach Andrews called me into his office. "You know," he said, "I didn't think you were going to play in the Emerald Bowl. I wasn't sure that you were going to have it all together. I thought you were going to tell me that you wanted to sit out."

"Once you all took me in, that was it."

"I wouldn't have been mad if you'd sat out. What happened to you was as strange as it was powerful. It was hard for me too."

Coach Andrews treated me like family. He cared more about my Christian walk than football. Our faith took precedence. What I experienced that night in Denny's was more significant than football. Coach understood that.

Knowing that I had that support carried over into my relationships with my teammates. Over the years at FSU, our bonds strengthened. I became a member of Kappa Alpha Psi fraternity with one of my best friends on the team. I still communicate with most of my teammates. These guys mean a lot to me. Marcus Simms has younger brothers and cousins interested in medicine, and I've allowed them to shadow me at Massachusetts General Hospital. It's a true brotherhood at Florida State.

The 2% Way prepared me to be the football player and the man I needed to become. I arrived at Florida State as a freshman with big-time talent and dreams of playing in the NFL. The 2% Way showed me how to achieve my goals. Coach Andrews brought this ethos into my life and unlocked my potential beyond the football field. The 2% Way shaped my approach toward faith, academics, my family life, and my relationships with friends. It's the foundational tool I use to work on each one of those aspects of my life.

I knew that if I took small steps to steadily improve, the world would be open to me. The 2% Way allowed me to go into a lab and study human mesenchymal stem cells in the bio-chem laboratory to see if they proliferate differently in different microenvironments. While I was still in college, it gave me the tools to drive six hours to Okeechobee, Florida, to teach a class on anti-obesity and high blood pressure to Native American children on the reservation. I counseled this underserved population on nutrition and healthy choices, hoping that someday one of these fine young people would go on to make a difference in the world.

That's a big part of why I wrote this book: hoping that sharing this method will help people achieve their full potential. You can use the 2% Way to improve any aspect of your life. Many of us have closed the doors of opportunity because we're not taking the small steps necessary to reach our goals. The 2% Way will take you to the point where you can open those doors and see what's out there for your life.

Chapter 4

THE COLOSSUS OF RHODES

Since the day I read Dr. Carson's *Gifted Hands* at age twelve, I've kept a running journal of my goals. Sometimes they are short notes: snaps of inspiration from my subconscious. Others take the form of detailed lists that outline a series of small steps toward important milestones. In my youth, I returned to this journal often, amending my goals as they matured alongside me.

At the end of my freshman year at FSU, I opened the worn notebook and ran my finger down the page, feeling the deep indentations my pen marks had made, tracing the timeline of my aspirations. *Be a #1 recruit. Graduate high school a year early. Make All-American. 4.0 GPA. Ball Out.*

Check. Check. Check. Check. Check.

On its own line, below these entries were two words in all caps and circled with red pen: *RHODES SCHOLAR.*

I'd written this entry when I was sixteen while walking around Princeton University on a fall day. The Ivy League campus sat across the street from the Hun School, and I would escape to its stone pathways lined with white magnolias when I needed a breather from Hun's unfriendly eyes. A calm settled on me there—this was the sort of institution that nurtured young men like me, young men who filled their notebooks with dreams they might someday make realities. I liked watching students clutch their books as if they were valuable jewels. That day, I was walking near the football stadium when I saw a shimmer of bronze in the autumn light. There stood a statue of Bill Bradley, the Princeton basketball legend who went on to become an NBA Hall of Famer and a US Senator from New Jersey. On the plaque below his name, I read the two words that would change the course of my life: Rhodes Scholar.

I had a feeling akin to the one I had when I stood in front of Pompey's golden statue back in the Bahamas. Here was a man forever enshrined in metal who had successfully traveled the road I hoped to walk. Bradley was the Associated Press Player of the Year in college basketball *and* a Rhodes Scholar.

Back in my dorm at Hun, I researched the Rhodes Scholarship. It is the oldest and most celebrated international fellowship in the world, established by British mining magnate Cecil John Rhodes. An imperialist with a racist past in South Africa, Rhodes wouldn't have wanted someone who looked like me at Oxford, which made me want to earn it that much more. Each year thirty-two students from the United States are selected as Rhodes Scholars through a decentralized process representing the fifty states. Bill Bradley had won it in 1965. One item in Bradley's biography caught my eye. Because of the scholarship, he had delayed starting his NBA career for two years. He decided to put academics above basketball. It took courage to sacrifice the acclaim and adoration of playing for the New York Knicks in Madison Square Garden to study in the quiet solitude of a library at Oxford. It was a choice I knew I might have to make one day.

Now, toward the end of freshman year at FSU, it was time to activate my goal. I would need to apply the 2% Way to make it through the rigorous selection process. The criteria that Mr. Rhodes outlined in his will still guide selection committees. His will outlines four standards by which aspiring Rhodes Scholars are judged:

1. his literary and scholastic attainments
2. his fondness of and success in manly outdoor sports such as cricket football and the like
3. his qualities of manhood truth courage devotion to duty sympathy for the protection of the weak kindliness unselfishness and fellowship and
4. his exhibition during school days of moral force of character and of instincts to lead and to take an interest in his schoolmates for those latter attributes will be likely in after-life to guide him to esteem the performance of public duty as his highest aim.[1]

My goals have always consumed me, but this was a challenge I didn't yet have the tools to face. To hit these lofty ideals, I would have to develop a new plan of action. It wasn't enough to say to myself, "I'm going to do this." I needed to create a blueprint for success. Once again, I returned to my journal of goals.

1. Find mentors who can aid in the process.
2. Differentiate myself from the other candidates.
3. Apply the 2% Way to each aspect of my candidacy.
4. Don't let pressure sabotage you.

The last item on the list troubled me. I once did an interview with *ESPN* magazine in which the reporter asked, "What do you struggle with most?" Without hesitation, I replied, "The thing that has been my biggest enemy in this world has been pressure. The pressure is tough, man. I'm not gonna lie. It's the hardest part. Easily."[2]

Pressure has been a constant in my life since the moment I started succeeding. Some of it is self-imposed. Not every kid decides in middle school to be a neurosurgeon and an NFL player. But most of it came from external forces. As soon as people see that you shine, they expect more from you. *Myron needs to make ten tackles this game. Myron needs to set the example. Myron cannot fail.*

The Rhodes Scholarship added more steam to this pressure cooker. I would be competing against the best students in the country. Part of me wondered, "Am I truly as gifted a student as I am an athlete? Have people been humoring me so that I'll continue to ball out on the field?" Doubt crept in and compounded the pressure.

How could I combat these feelings of inadequacy? As I pondered this, another question from that same interview with ESPN popped into my head: "Are you chasing what you want or, because you are competitive and driven, are you chasing whatever happens to be society's agreed upon definition of greatness?"

I had answered, "I'd say it has partly to do with the perceived notion that the Rhodes Scholarship and the NFL are outstanding achievements and agreed upon by the vast majority. To me, it's the highest level of my passions, my individual passions, in academics and athletics."[3]

Now, as I look back on my answer, I didn't think that was what I wanted to say about my attitude toward achievement. Pressure came from trying to conform to "the vast majority" of people's opinions, "the agreed upon definition of greatness." Having people take notice is a part of the achievement, but if that's all you focus on, you're doomed to live a life in which success depends on the opinions of others. I decided then and there that I would build my Rhodes application with what mattered to me, not what pleased or impressed others. If I weren't selected, I would still have a foundation on which to stand. The pressure would still be there, but it would be pressure I put on myself.

I opened my goal list and amended the last entry:

4. ~~Don't let the pressure get in the way.~~
4. Let your burning desire to do something meaningful destroy pressure. Let your actions be driven by your expectations for yourself, not external forces.

With my soul-level intentions set, it was time to put my goals into motion. Number one on my list: mentors. I'd planted the seeds for mentorship during my recruiting trips. At Florida State, I'd met Garrett Johnson, a Black man from Tampa who had won a Rhodes. He was an All-American shot-putter, a two-time national champion, the epitome of a student-athlete. He had researched migration patterns and poverty in Haiti and was an aide to Florida governor Jeb Bush. He became my big brother on campus. He checked in on me every week, even though he had finished his coursework. We'd eat breakfast together and talk over how I should prepare for the Rhodes Scholarship. He had his hands on me, molding me, making sure that I took the suitable courses in school and joined the right community service activities. Garrett advised me to get involved in the Office of National Fellowships at Florida State. It was a program dedicated to postgraduate fellowship opportunities, and the man who headed up the office was named Jody Spooner.

Jody ran what he called salons, held in a posh room at FSU's law school. "It's reserved for the trustees, but I've got the key," he told me with a wink. Monday evenings after football practice, seven other students also interested in postgraduate fellowships and I would debate there. Jody and Garrett introduced topics for us to discuss. "Poverty," Garrett would say. We learned to speak and argue. We learned how to elucidate our thoughts eloquently.

The salons were the first time I was challenged intellectually in a formalized or professional setting. The debates were a form of competition in which my physical ability was of no use to me. I followed the rules of civil discourse and was obliged to support my beliefs with convincing arguments. No one was crowned the victor, but those debates focused my thoughts and expanded my mind.

During this time, another guiding voice was Dr. Sally Karioth, a longtime faculty member of the Florida State University College of Nursing. I met her my sophomore year during a six-week study abroad in London, where she taught one of the program's most popular courses, called "Death, the Individual, and the Family." Daddy had accompanied me on the trip—the Bahamas is a British Commonwealth, and going to England is a pilgrimage all our compatriots try to make in their lifetime. At orientation Dr. Karioth came up to us and asked, "And who is this?"

"This is my father, Whitney Rolle," I said.

"You're the only one with a parent here," she said, gesturing toward the rest of the students.

"I'm just making sure he's all right in a new country," Daddy replied.

Dr. Karioth later told me that was the moment she took an interest in me. That I would not be left to drift alone abroad was indicative of our family and the role they expected of me. She and I grew very close that trip. Originally from Wisconsin, she had been a Green Bay Packers cheerleader. She told me many times, "Life is what you make it. Make the best of it." Dr. Karioth took me to *The Lion King*, my first play. Afterward, walking the streets of London, she asked me what I thought the play's message was.

"If Simba had just listened to his daddy, everything would have been straight," I replied.

She burst out laughing. "Most people would say Simba needed to become his own man."

"Nope."

"Myron, you'll always be a Rolle before anything else," she said, still giggling.

Fine by me, I thought.

When it was time to apply for the Rhodes Scholarship in my junior year, I talked to another mentor, T. K. Wetherell, FSU's president. I showed him my blueprint for success in my goal journal, and he pointed to #2: Set yourself apart from the other applicants. "That's the key," he said. "Yes, football will help, but you need something more."

"I'm premed; I'm going to be a doctor one day," I said. "Maybe I can use that."

"We have a great relationship with the Seminole Tribe of Florida," he said. "How about reaching out to them?"

"Let me think about the health deficits that Native Americans may be experiencing," I replied.

And so I researched, applying the 2% Way. What health challenges were the Seminole Tribe facing? I learned that obesity, hypertension, diabetes, smoking, alcoholism, and prescription drug abuse were endemic to the tribe. Even though they had some money because the tribe owned the Hard Rock Casinos in Florida, they still dealt with the effects of the cultural genocide their ancestors experienced. Poverty, poor nutrition, substandard housing, and inadequate access to health care adversely affected the health of the tribe members.

I went down to the Brighton Seminole Indian Reservation, near Lake Okeechobee's northwest shore, and met with the matriarch and the chief of the tribe. They gave me their blessing to institute an interactive health intervention based on these conversations and my personal research. I met with the school principal and spoke to all the students about living well, goal setting, and keeping cultural customs alive while being healthy.

But something happened when I was down there. I wanted to give more than a speech. I wanted to effect change in their lives. I created an anti-obesity program called Our Way to Health. The idea was to use a team-based approach to develop different health-related activities in physical education classes. The students were placed on a team, and all the activities centered on healthy lifestyle choices. The goal was to integrate health education into a game-type format that involved physical activities. In one game, there were various hoops with different answers to questions. A team would answer a health-related question, then sprint to place a ball in the circle with the correct answer.

They were also given roles to mimic the hierarchy of their tribal government. One kid named Layton Thomas took a special interest in the program and earned the title chairman of the board.

I created the health curriculum and the games using the 2% Way. I knew these kids had a long way to go with their health but that they could make minor improvements if we provided them with incentives. I decided to use competition to drive that incremental progress. The team that won would get to come up on the field with me at halftime of a Florida State football game and be introduced on the jumbotron to eighty-five thousand screaming Seminole fans and a live TV audience of millions. Layton Thomas told me that it was one of the best moments of his life. It was also one of my proudest moments. No matter if I won the Rhodes or not, I would look back on this day with soul-level satisfaction. I still smile when I think about the looks on those kids' faces.

Today many of those kids have maintained their health, and I've stayed connected to their lives, aiding as I can. One student went on to be one of the most successful music producers in South Florida. Others went back to their tribe to become educators, leading the next generation as much-needed mentors. Ripple effects like this are proof of the change we can produce when we inspire marginalized communities.

This program, my athletic background, and my continued commitment to my academics allowed me to become a Rhodes finalist at Florida State. The next step was to pass mock interviews at FSU before I could be recommended to the national Rhodes committee. I walked into a classroom in one of the College of Health and Human Sciences buildings at Florida State wearing a black suit, a white shirt, and a red bow tie. Six prestigious faculty members sat around a polished wooden table. I did not know a single person on the committee. The seat at the head of the table was empty. I sat down.

The first question was about football. I answered as if I were speaking to a sports reporter. I was jovial, even cavalier. Those character traits had made me a media darling with the sportswriters—but not here. The rules of the game were different in this room.

Then came the question that burned me like a quarterback

throwing a big touchdown pass to the receiver I was supposed to be covering. "What is one of the major challenges you've seen in the Bahamas, and how would you fix it?"

"One of the major problems is gang violence," I replied. "And most of the violence is happening because of the Haitian immigrants that are coming into the country. They were in gangs in Haiti, and they left Haiti for the Bahamas, but they brought their gangs and their violence with them."

A committee member pushed me on my response, as he should have. "Oh, so the reason why the Bahamas has problems is because of the Haitians? They're bad people?"

"Well, they're not bad people, but you know, the crime rate has gone up since they've come," I said. I stumbled over my words. "Haitians, sometimes they're unruly and sometimes have this voodoo that they do."

The moment the word *voodoo* came out of my mouth, I knew I had dug myself a hole that there was no climbing out of. I realize now that when I made those statements about Haiti, it was a regurgitation of what I had heard from older generations in the Bahamas. Unfortunately, some Bahamians feel that way, and that's a shortcoming of our society. But some of those conversations bled into church cookouts and into my young ears. When I got stuck on a tough question, my amygdala, a collection of cells near the base of the brain attached to associations and responses to them, or emotional memories, told me, *This sounds right.*

But it wasn't right. I knew that as I said those words. I didn't hold those beliefs and do not. My love for the Caribbean, for all people, does not take borders into account. It crosses beliefs, customs, and traditions, including the Haitian ones. Many of my generation of Bahamians share in this belief and consider Haitians part of our Caribbean family. Just like in America, it is up to the youth to root out older prejudices, which exist in every society, in order to move the needle on progress.

I walked out of that room like I was walking to the sideline after being burned for a touchdown during a practice in July. Sweat poured down my neck. I loosened my bow tie and sat down on the first chair I saw. Jody walked up to me. "I think I'm in trouble," I told him.

Jody nodded. He knew the score. When you are a defensive back and give up a touchdown pass, the whole stadium knows it was you. Later that night, he called to break the news. "What did they say?" I asked.

"They said you were woefully underprepared and not ready to move on," Jody told me. He was as blunt as my defensive backs coach.

"So that's it?" I asked.

"They're not inclined to put you forward, but they are willing to give you another chance," he said. "They think you have potential."

Another chance. Potential. Hope. If I applied the 2% Way every day, I could improve enough by the time of the second mock interview that I might stand a chance. I had blown the coverage, but I could recover if I applied the 2% Way.

Every day after football, I would practice answering interview questions with Dr. Karioth. She would read *USA Today* or the *New York Times* and say, "Okay, Myron. I've got seven questions for you." She would ask me about anything. And I would have to answer every question and improve 2 percent each day.

Garrett Johnson, the shot-putting Rhodes Scholar, played his part. One day I was driving when I got a call from him. "You got time for a mock interview? I have some friends on speakerphone." I pulled over into a U-Haul parking lot, and the five Rhodes Scholars Garrett had on the line peppered me with questions. When I fumbled an answer, they corrected me. We went back and forth for almost an hour, steadily improving my responses through insight from those who knew the process better than anyone. It was the 2% Way at work in a U-Haul parking lot.

So I prepared for my second shot. This time, I put on a gray suit and white shirt with a yellow tie. I ditched the red bow tie; it wasn't "me." I again sat at the head of the table in the same chair, but I knew this time would be different. I wasn't nervous. The 2% Way had prepared me. I answered question after question calmly and confidently. I focused on trying to make every answer 2 percent better than the last.

About a week after my second interview, Jody Spooner called me. "You made it," he told me. "You're a finalist."

I was elated; my hard work had paid off. My final interview was on November 22, 2008. "As long as it's not a Saturday," I joked.

"Wait," he said. I could hear the rustling of his desk calendar as he flipped pages. "Oh no . . ."

November 22 was a Saturday, the same day as an away game against Maryland. The interview was in Birmingham, Alabama. I imagined the string of expletives Coach Andrews would let out when I told him. But now I had a bargaining chip in my back pocket. Every college desperately wants to produce a Rhodes Scholar. It's the ultimate badge of honor.

Birmingham was only a two-hour flight from Maryland. If I took one of FSU's booster's private planes, I might be able to make it to the game in time to play. When I ran my proposition by T. K. Wetherell, he cocked an eyebrow and said, "You better win the game and the scholarship. And you better parachute onto the fifty-yard line."

Wetherell needed me as much as I needed his private plane. FSU was embroiled in a series of athletic scandals. Shortly after the Rhodes finalists were announced, Wetherell told the *New York Times* that I was carrying Florida State's reputation on my back. The media picked up the story and ran with it. Jeremy Schaap of ESPN did an *Outside the Lines* segment, interviewing a couple of my teammates and my head coach, Bobby Bowden. Schaap looked right into the camera and asked, "Will Myron win the Rhodes?" His next question was, "Will he make it to the game on time?"

"Wish I knew, Jeremy," I said to the television. ESPN ran this *Outside the Lines* daily leading up to the game on Saturday. It was an effective strategy—word got out. I could hear the chatter. *Is he going to do it? Is it going to happen?* My phone was clogged with texts from anyone and everyone I'd ever met. My pastors called me, praying; family from the Bahamas called me, saying, "I saw you on TV, you okay, boy?" My cousin Samari Rolle, himself no stranger to high-pressure situations—he played in the 1999 Super Bowl—checked in, telling me, "You're a Rolle, you got this." It was nice to get a call from someone who could relate to what I was going through.

But believe it or not, the pressure never got to me. I had crossed that off my list months before. I got one final boost from my teammates the Thursday before I left for Birmingham—during practice they all laid their hands on my shoulders and prayed for me. Then I hopped in a car with Dr. Karioth and headed for Alabama.

On the Saturday that would decide the course of my life, I woke up in my hotel room and prepared like I was getting ready for the game against Maryland. Two percent better on every response or two percent better on every play. It's the same winning recipe. A Rhodes Scholarship was within reach of a young Black man from the Bahamas. The 2% Way had gotten me to this point. It was time to bring this one back to the house.

I took a long shower as I did before games. I envisioned myself making a bunch of plays on the football field. I imagined myself answering all the questions precisely, with the same poise and confidence I displayed on the football field. I remembered all the advice my mentors had given me. I put on my suit and boarded a bus that took me to the interview facility.

I was the second to last candidate to interview. I sat in a room waiting and watching an LSU football game. Seeing the LSU players on national television, knowing that I was as good as any of them, I felt like I couldn't lose. It seemed as if I was floating that day. When

I look back on it now, I see I wasn't floating. I was lifted up by the love and support of my family, my friends, my mentors, my coaches, and my teammates. I had used the 2% Way to prepare me for this opportunity. Each person along the way helped me become 2 percent better, and pretty soon, it all started to add up.

Dr. Karioth had told me that the judges might interview me more than once. I sat there, my phone buzzing with texts from family and friends. I watched two candidates get called back for a second time. They would award only two scholarships in my district, and I hadn't even interviewed yet.

At that point, doubt could have crept in. I could have said to myself, "They are calling those students back just to confirm that they want them." Instead, I told myself, "Don't think of it as a bad thing. They are just being thorough. What is going on in that room has nothing to do with you." Waiting my turn, I felt confident. All my preparation was responsible for that calm. It wasn't overconfidence—I wasn't at all sure I would be chosen. But I knew I would be comfortable with whatever happened in that room. I am comfortable with being the Myron I know I am *and* the Myron everyone thinks I can be. "If it's not good enough for y'all," I thought, "then oh well. But if it is, welcome to Oxford."

At 12:50 p.m., a man in a black suit came out and said, "Myron, come on back." I stood and walked into the room. In front of me was the same setup I had seen in my mock interviews, only with different faces. In the front of the room was Drayton Nabers Jr., a lawyer and former chief justice of the Alabama Supreme Court. To his left was Ralph Smith, the head of the legal counsel for the University of Alabama system. Four other judges, all professors I'd researched, fanned out in a semicircle. "Take a seat, Myron," Justice Nabers said. This was it.

"Tell us about the mentorship that you did for Black kids in Tallahassee," Nabers began. "Why was that important to you?"

"These young men and women of color need to see an example

of what education and knowledge can do," I said. My words were smooth. I did not hesitate. "The more examples that they can see of excellence and success, the more possible those avenues become for them. I wanted to set an example for people who face some of the same challenges I did because of the color of our skin."

Ralph Smith scribbled something on his yellow legal pad and raised a finger in my direction. "You're going to graduate from FSU in two and a half years, Myron. Why did you want to graduate so early? You didn't want to double major?"

I hadn't expected that question. I decided to be honest. "I got through it so fast because I was always on campus," I said. "I didn't have time to be anywhere else. When you are part of a football program like FSU's, you are always training, always lifting weights, always at the ready. I figured I'm already here; I might as well take as many classes as I can. To be honest with you, my goal was to get to the National Football League after my junior year and to have my degree in hand before I did that. I guess the NFL was my backup plan in case I didn't become a Rhodes Scholar."

Luckily, I was in a room full of judges from the South. They all understood how important football is to the culture down here—most of them were fans themselves.

Then they asked me, "Myron, what three books do you have on your nightstand?" Inside, I smiled. Garrett had told me that they had asked him this question and had asked it of every other Rhodes candidate he knew. I'd thought about my answer for weeks. All the books had to speak to my core values. They all had to matter in some significant way.

"The first is the Bible," I began. "Always first. That grounds me in my Christian faith, reminds me of how important it is to stay connected to Christ. The second book is *Running for My Life* by Warrick Dunn. Warrick was a running back for Florida State and the Atlanta Falcons. His mother was a police officer who was shot and killed in the line of duty. Warrick Dunn went to Angola

Prison, where the man who shot his mother was incarcerated, and spoke with that man. He forgave him for shooting his mother when he was a young boy. Now Warrick builds homes for single-parent households across the country. That book speaks to my desire to use a football life as a medium to change the world. The last book I have on my nightstand is *Mountains beyond Mountains* by Tracy Kidder. It traces physician and anthropologist Paul Farmer's life, focusing on his work fighting tuberculosis in Haiti. Farmer treated infectious diseases in the developing world in a way that was rooted in social justice. It speaks to my interest in medical anthropology and global health."

Thank you, Garrett, I said silently to myself when I had finished. The room seemed responsive enough to my answers, but they weren't letting up their poker faces. The last question they asked was: "President-elect Barack Obama is quite young. You are also a young man who is going to try to change the world through health care. What would you tell Barack Obama right now if you could call him on the phone and tell him how to fix health care in this country?"

"Well, health care has been a difficult issue for a long time," I said. "No administration has solved it. It's unlikely to be resolved even in Obama's administration. Nevertheless, I would tell Barack Obama to get the smartest people around you, who know more about this issue than you and can provide you with the requisite insights. In this way, you can make well-informed choices for the majority of people in the country." I paused for a moment. Then I said, "Then I'd tell him to pray about it, my brother, pray about it."

The steely silence in the room broke into laughter. Justice Nabers took off his glasses and wiped his eyes with the back of his hand. "I got them," I thought. "I got these old stuffy professors to laugh."

Then, just like that, it was over. It was in God's hands now. The same black-suited gentleman who had led me into the room now took me back to the waiting room. When he opened the door, he gave me a quick wink and smiled. That was the moment I knew I had won.

I still had to wait for two hours while the judges deliberated. I didn't want to smile in the waiting room, but inside I beamed for that entire time. I knew I had it in the bag, but more than that, I had left no part of myself behind during the process.

All the candidates stood when the judges came back into the room. And then they said my name. It sounded sweeter than ESPN mentioning my name on *SportsCenter*. Myron Rolle, Rhodes Scholar. "That's got a nice ring to it," I thought.

Then things started happening in fast-forward. A flurry of hand-shakes. An interview with a local newspaper where I hardly knew what I was saying. A contract was placed in front of me; I signed on the line that said "Rhodes Scholar." When the crowd subsided for a moment, I reached for my phone. I didn't even want to look at how many texts had piled up. There was only one number I needed to call.

Mummy answered on the first ring. "Tell us!"

"I won," I said. That was all I got out. The phone exploded with noise. I couldn't get a word in. They passed the phone around to everybody: Daddy took it first and told me he was so proud of me, that he loved me. All my brothers came on the phone and shouted joyful praise into the phone.

Daddy got back on the line. "We're driving to the stadium right now," he said. "We'll see you there."

That's when I remembered the Maryland game. I went back to the hotel, took off my suit, and put on my garnet-and-gold Florida State travel gear. I picked up my bags and walked out the door. Dr. Karioth was waiting to drive me to the Birmingham Airport. We pulled up, and she hustled me out of the car.

I rushed through security and was ushered onto a tarmac. I saw a private jet idling on the runway. *Thank you, T. K.* I sprinted up the stairs. On the plane, a bevy of reporters greeted me like a conquer-ing hero: *Sports Illustrated*, the *Chronicle of Higher Education*, and the *Tallahassee Democrat*. A photographer snapped pictures. T. K.

Wetherell had made sure Florida State would get a photo op with its new Rhodes Scholar. That was fine by me. I knew nobody rides on a private jet for free. I fielded all their questions effortlessly: I was already in interview mode. But then the *Sports Illustrated* reporter asked me a question I wasn't prepared for.

"How do you think this will affect your draft status?" he asked.

"Let me get back to you on that one," I said. "Right now I just want to enjoy this moment."

"Fair enough," he said.

"Can I ask *you* something?" I asked the photographer as she snapped a picture of me that would soon be plastered all over *SportsCenter*.

"Shoot."

"Can I have half your lunch? I haven't eaten anything all day."

She laughed and split her turkey wrap with me.

I devoured the wrap, put in my headphones, and cued up Ice Cube's "It Was a Good Day" on my iPod. The minute that g-funk baseline coursed through my ears, I was able to relax a bit. *Juss wakin' up in tha mornin', gotta thank God. I don't know, but today seems kinda odd.* Next I put on Frank Sinatra's "It Was a Very Good Year." Exhaustion took over, and I fell asleep as Ol' Blue Eyes crooned: *When I was twenty-one, it was a very good year.*

I woke up when we touched down at Thurgood Marshall Airport. A police escort rushed me to Byrd Stadium. A crowd of people parted ways as our vehicle zoomed through the gate. We were so close to the field, I could see the garnet and gold of my teammate's uniforms on the sidelines.

When I got to the locker room, the first person I saw was Mummy. I'd never seen a look of pride quite like the one on her face that day. She threw her arms around my waist—she's not a tall woman—and said, "I love you, I love you, I love you."

Jack Arute from ESPN was right on her heels. Arute announced into his microphone, "And the newest Rhodes Scholar has arrived.

How do you feel?" He turned his mic to me, a camera light bright in my face. "I don't even know what to say right now," I said. "I'm speechless; it's amazing."

ESPN's cameras followed me to my locker. My jersey was set up, and my pads were right beside my cleats. I got taped up and began to undress—following the same routine I did before every game— trying to ignore the choreographed whirlwind around me. I looked over at the ESPN cameraman and said, "Hey, man, I'm about to take off my pants." He backed off sheepishly.

When I emerged dressed in my game gear, FSU's athletic director, Randy Spetman, grabbed me by the shoulder. "Hey, Myron, before you go, give your daddy a hug. And then I want you to run through the cheerleaders." They had this all set up in advance. Florida State knew what they were doing. This was their moment to shine as well as mine.

I was more than happy to hug my daddy. I grabbed him with all I had. As we put our arms around each other, I remembered the safety of his embrace I had felt many years ago as I watched my brother Whitney play football in Galloway. I had used the strength he had transferred to me and the 2% Way to deliver on the promise of that embrace.

"Go," Daddy said. "It's already the second quarter."

I ran through a line of cheerleaders onto the field. The PA announcer boomed, "And now entering the field, the newest Rhodes Scholar, Myron Rolle."

The entire stadium rose as one, even the Maryland fans, to give me a standing ovation. It was phenomenal. I remember the game when the Seminole Tribe kids stood at the fifty-yard line with the biggest smiles on their faces. The smile on my face was as wide as theirs had been.

The cameras followed me to the sidelines. My teammates slapped me on the back, yelling, "Whatchu talkin' 'bout, three! Whatchu talking about, three!" One of my boys, Dekoda Watson, moved next to me on the bench, saying, "You won? Let me sit next to you so I can get some camera time too."

When I finished warming up, Coach Andrews said, "Hey, Myron, congratulations. Ready to go?"

"Yes, sir. I'm ready."

"Well, get your a— in there." I'd never been so happy to be sworn at in my life.

The back-judge referee patted me on the butt and said, "Congratulations on that Rhodes Scholarship, son."

"Thank you very much, sir. I appreciate it."

"Doesn't mean you're getting any free calls, though."

"Wouldn't dream of it, sir."

The next play, I closed on a receiver named Darrius Heyward-Bey running a slant route, and tackled him. "Hey, man, you won the scholarship?" Darrius asked as we ran back toward our respective huddles.

"Yeah, man, I won."

"That's big-time, bro."

We won the game 37–3, the first time we beat Maryland during my time at Florida State. At the end of the game, my teammates doused me with a Gatorade cooler of ice water. I didn't even feel the cold. I was still floating.

I was still floating that night at the hotel with my teammates as we celebrated FSU's win. "President is gonna be the president," they kept saying as we bumped music late into the night. I was still floating on the plane ride back to Florida, still floating when the team bus pulled up to FSU's stadium in Tallahassee.

I don't think I landed on the ground until I was alone, walking home. I lived a four- or five-minute walk from the stadium. I always walked back from practice and games on a little tree-lined path. I set off alone in the dark: there was only a flicker of light on the pathway. The silence and solitude of the night settled on me.

That's when I knew that something big had happened. My life

had changed. I didn't realize it when I won the scholarship. I didn't realize it on the private jet or the police escort. I didn't realize it when I was on the field at Maryland and tens of thousands of people were cheering for me. But on that silent walk home alone on a dimly lit path, I realized my life would never be the same.

I'm aware that my story is atypical for a Black student-athlete. It doesn't have to be. I'm not talking about the private plane or the cheerleaders. All that is just window dressing. I'm talking about having it all. With the proper support and the 2% Way, student-athletes can break through the stereotypes that limit us.

When I stood up for myself and said, *This is who I want to be. This is where I want to go*, FSU helped. They understood my aspirations and their role in helping me achieve my goals. When I talk to young student-athletes, I tell them to write their own playbook. You have more leverage than you think you do. You have the power to say, "I want to pursue my dreams beyond athletics. I want to help Seminole children lead healthier lives. I want to be a neurosurgeon. I want to be a Rhodes Scholar."

Chapter 5

32 / 32

Shortly after I won the Rhodes, I posted a poll to Twitter.

What would you do in my position?

> Enter the NFL draft.
> Go to Oxford.

Most responses urged me to go to the National Football League. "Think about all that money," one follower commented. When I brought this question to my FSU teammates over breakfast at the Waffle House, they looked at me, puzzled. "The NFL has been the dream since we were jits," they said. "Not all of us can go to the league. Get in there while you can."

By some estimates, I would sacrifice as much as $8 million by skipping the 2009 draft. I'd always viewed money as a means to fund my future goals in medicine, and it was tempting to have that lifelong security. Yet Oxford and the Rhodes Scholarship was a tremendous opportunity that I couldn't get back. The scholarship committee had been clear: I could not postpone.

As I wrestled with this decision, I continued to check my Twitter page. One comment, posted by a Black student at Leon High School in Tallahassee, read, "Go to England. Take a risk, and you'll inspire others. You can come back to football." That mindset tipped the scales. If I made this choice, I could show young people, especially young Black people, that I valued education more than money.

I didn't see my situation as a conundrum. I had all the tools to be a pro football player *and* an academic scholar. Success in one area didn't have to preclude the other. I'd been at the top level of performance at every level in football and believed I could be a star in the National Football League. Why would taking a year and a half to broaden my horizons change that?

I set a new goal. Every November, thirty-two students are awarded Rhodes Scholarships. Every April, thirty-two young men are picked in the first round of the NFL draft. There has never been any overlap between the two groups. When I returned from England in eighteen months, I would be the first.

Nobody lets you be the first at something without some resistance. In January 2009, four months after winning the Rhodes, I was interviewed by Chris McKendry for *SportsCenter*. She leaned over the desk and asked, "Myron, are you going to the NFL, or are you going to Oxford?"

"The opportunity to attend Oxford next year as a Rhodes Scholar was one that I couldn't pass up," I said. "But I feel that my skills and my talent will surface once I go to the combine next year and continue to work out to stay in shape and continue with the same path as I was at Florida State."

When the accompanying *ESPN* piece ran, the headline read "Florida State Safety Myron Rolle Will Study at Oxford Instead of Entering This Year's NFL Draft."

Instead. The word glared through the sentence. Within days, I heard from NFL teams and scouts that they were worried I wasn't serious about football. "This decision will hurt your draft stock," they warned. "Here's a guy we don't feel cares about the sport," I read on one scouting report. Not serious about football? It was frustrating to know that in stadium offices, men I had never met were constructing a narrative that ran contrary to the facts of my life. The chatter was still just chatter, but with media attention and enough raised eyebrows, chatter can quickly morph into reality.

If I fell in the draft, I stood to lose millions of dollars. There's a reason why the first and second rounds are on day one of the draft when millions watch at home. A first-round pick is an investment. When a franchise has laid a good deal of money on the table, they give a player years to develop. Even second-round picks often have long lives in the league. But if you fall beyond that, you had better perform, or else you'll be clearing out your locker not long after you set down your cleats. And when you take a year off, that scrutiny is magnified.

Though I tried not to consider it, there was also the possibility that commissioner Roger Goodell would never call my name, and I'd be left sitting next to Mummy and Daddy with my head in my hands. Slight cracks appeared in the self-confidence I had built through years of work. Would I never intercept a pass in the NFL because of the leap I was about to take?

But I'd made my decision, and once you do that, you can't question it. You have to maximize the opportunities in your new path. Becoming a Rhodes Scholar unlocks access to people an immigrant kid from New Jersey would typically never have the chance to meet. One immediately joins a fraternity of individuals such as George Stephanopoulos, Rachel Maddow, Ronan Farrow, Pete Dawkins, Bill Bradley, and Susan Rice. My phone started ringing and didn't stop: President Bill Clinton's and Senator Cory Booker's offices reached out and scheduled meetings.

Writer Aldous Huxley once wrote, "Most human beings have an almost infinite capacity for taking things for granted."[1] If I was giving up a roster spot in the NFL, I couldn't take a moment of the following year for granted. "Just take it two percent at a time," I told myself. I resolved to grab a fistful of knowledge from each person I was about to meet and apply it to my journey overseas.

The Bahamas, of course, were the first to big me up. I had hardly uttered the words "I accept" when the government called to ask if I would give a talk to the student body of the College of the Bahamas. They planned to broadcast the speech on their national network on Majority Rule Day, which celebrates the Bahamas gaining fair representation and equality in 1967. Prime Minister Perry Christie stood in front of the members of Parliament, watching my speech. After that visit, they put me on a national stamp commemorating Bahamas's forty years of freedom.

I held the stamp on the tip of my finger. Small as it was, it connected me to our national story and our colonial history, symbolic of my small etching into the Bahamian legacy that Pompey had begun. His tools had been rebellion and courage. Mine were academics and athletics, but each of us strived to further the autonomy of Black people.

Over the next five months, I met with people who, pre-Rhodes, had been figures on my television screen or I had read about in books. At his library in Little Rock, Arkansas, President Bill Clinton asked me to attend a summit centered on combating sexual violence toward women in Congo. "Young leaders make up this group," he told me, "but you'll be one of the youngest." I met with New Jersey Senator Cory Booker at his office in Newark. Sitting in my living room in Galloway, I'd seen him on the news staging a ten-day hunger strike to draw attention to urban development issues in his city. He'd studied theology at Oxford and asked me about my plans for the future as they related to my faith. I launched into a monologue about how I planned to apply the knowledge gained at Oxford to the next five years of my life.

"If you want God to laugh, tell him your plans," Senator Booker said when I took a moment to breathe.

"I put a lot of stock into plans," I replied.

"That's a good thing, but even if all those things don't happen for you, you're going to be working toward something," he said. "In the end, you'll go forward."

That conversation stoked my 2 percent flame before I left for England. I told myself, "Have thoughts and visions of where you want to be, grab that two percent every single day. And if it doesn't work out exactly as you planned it, that's okay because you've gone two percent farther than if you had stayed stagnant." I knew it wouldn't go exactly as I intended; I'd be in a new country.

I picked up my first brand partnership with Xenith, a helmet company interested in concussions, traumatic brain injury, and smart tech. I wanted to see the cutting-edge technology that could protect my brain because I would certainly need that knowledge as a neurosurgeon. On a conference call, the helmet company executives asked if I would like to meet a hero of mine.

"How could you do that?" I asked.

"We'll work it out. Can you meet us in New York?"

My mother and I drove to Manhattan, and there Xenith's executives shuttled us to a corporate office in Midtown. When the boardroom door swung open, there stood Bill Bradley. In person, he was almost as tall as his statue, the very same statue that had inspired my quest for a Rhodes that day on Princeton's campus. He dwarfed Mummy when he hugged her.

Bradley spoke in the easy way of a man who has done what he set out to do in life. And he still moved with the swagger of a Knick who brought New York two championships. "Get around to some different countries," he told me. "But take it more seriously than I did with the books."

When much is expected of you, the people you look up to rarely tell you to have fun. Street agents in the club tell you to kick back, but I knew better than to listen to that source of information. Hearing those words from a Hall of Famer who became a senator gave me the green light to be a human while I was overseas. If giants like Bill Bradley believed in me, I could reach into this new world with an open mind. Experience, not expectation, would be my engine.

During this period of furious attention, I showed up to winter FSU practice ready to ball, keeping an eye out for NFL scouts who might be checking to see if I was still "committed to football," a concept I find ridiculous to this day. I was on the FSU practice field with a chip on my shoulder like I was still that high school kid from New Jersey traveling to Oklahoma trying to earn my first scholarship. Let them try to discount my play. I wouldn't give them a chance.

One afternoon in February, I had just finished practice and was sitting in my car blasting Plies—those Florida boys had convinced me of the charms of Southern hip-hop—when I got a call from a Chicago number I didn't recognize. Typically, I don't answer unknown numbers, but something told me to pick up the phone.

"Is this Myron Rolle?" asked an older voice that sounded like a deacon from a Black church. The oration of pastors and deacons in Black churches, especially older Baptist churches, has a singsongy-ness to it. When they speak, their voice trembles, as if they're about to burst into music. They often do.

I shut off the Machel Montano real quick.

"Yes, sir," I said, reverting to my church manners.

"This is Reverend Jesse Jackson. I want to tell you something. You are a role model. You are a hero to so many of these young Black brothers. If Dr. King were alive today, he'd be very proud of you, son."

This was a man who had walked side by side with Dr. King. I put my hand to my head, telling myself to remember this moment and knowing I would never forget it.

Reverend Jackson told me he wanted to invest in my life and invited me to the Super Bowl in Tampa, Florida. We went to the Buccaneers facility, where the Steelers and the Cardinals were practicing. I saw behind the scenes of an experience I wanted for myself.

Anytime a reporter approached Reverend Jackson during the game, he would say, "I want you to meet Myron Rolle. This is the Rhodes Scholar; he's going to be a future NFL player." Just as Lorenzo Booker had when I was at Florida State, Reverend Jackson would always direct everyone's attention to me. "I want to make sure you all shine a light on this young brother," Reverend Jackson repeated all afternoon. "He's next. He's coming." That Reverend Jackson could recognize both sides of me—the athlete and the scholar—and not question my commitment to either made me feel seen.

From Reverend Jackson, I grabbed the affirmation that, as Black men in America, we are responsible to the youth who look to us to help them move in the right direction. Our conversations made me think about how I could apply the 2% Way to helping Black people. How could my personal improvements also bring their needs to the spotlight? That idea had always lived inside me; now, as I got ready to go overseas, it burned at the forefront of my mind. Black America needed leaders. Black America would still require leaders when I came home.

Reverend Jackson continued to mentor me as I prepared to leave for England. In our talks, he harkened back to Black leaders of the past, drawing a line between my present and their history of activism. He told me to study Shirley Chisholm, who was the first Black major-party candidate to run for president of the United States in 1972. We spoke on Fannie Lou Hamer, who was arrested and brutally beaten in 1963 for sitting in a "whites only" bus station restaurant in Winona, Mississippi. Instead of letting that hatred defeat her, she founded the Freedom Democratic Party, which challenged the local Democratic Party's efforts to block Black participation. "When you think about what to do with the opportunities the Rhodes will give you, think about these women," Reverend Jackson told me.

In April, the NFL draft came and went. I watched with my brother Cory as the first defensive back, Malcolm Jenkins, went off the board at fourteen to New Orleans. The next defensive back to go was Vontae Davis to Miami at twenty-five. An alternate reality of my life played out on the screen as Davis held up the Dolphins jersey and threw an arm over Roger Goodell.

"This is fuel," Cory said. "This year, Oxford. Next year you're going to be on that stage, crying in front of Mummy and Daddy."

"You think I'll cry?" I asked, punching him in the arm.

"Oh, I *know* you'll cry if you go in the first round. Daddy will too."

A few days before my flight, Cory and I packed our bags together. I was thankful Cory would be with me in Oxford; I needed my family by my side. He would be a living reminder of all that I had to accomplish when I got back home.

Along with new sets of suits and ties—my FSU sweats and hoodies weren't going to cut it in England—we packed my weight vest, parachute, ankle weights, and ladder. We brought the same equipment I would have brought to train for the NFL Combine. The last thing we put in the bag was a football. We both knew what it meant.

I turned to my faith to guide my last days in the States. I wanted to make the last time I went to church in America memorable. I would find a church in England, but it wouldn't be a Black American church.

My boyhood hero, the man who had inspired me to be a neurosurgeon, Dr. Ben Carson invited me to come to church with him on my final Sunday in America. Today, when I ask another Black physician why they went into medicine, they often cite Dr. Carson's *Gifted Hands* as the reason. That book was the catalyst that helped them find something they had not yet seen in themselves. I laugh when I hear that because it was my experience entirely. To write something that creates a commonality of experience among Black people and unlocks the potential within all of us is one of the highest forms of purpose.

After church, Dr. Carson gave me advice gleaned from a lifetime spent as a neurosurgeon. "Make sure you learn the names and the stories of the janitors, the people that work in the cafeteria," he said. "Doctors often move past them like they don't matter."

"I'll do that," I said.

"Be kind to them. Know them," he said. "You'll need friends beyond your attending."

● ● ●

Bon voyage. It was a fitting name for the inaugural week of the Rhodes, when I was whisked away to Washington, DC, where fifty scholars from North America congregated. That weekend, I met like-minded people who believed they would change the world. Among my first friends were Shad White, a passionate white Republican from Mississippi, and a young man named Abdul El-Sayed, who told me how he thought politics and morality could go hand in hand. A scholar named Chris Joseph recognized me—he had played football at UCLA. "Offensive line," he told me. "I blocked you in the Emerald Bowl. I thought you were going to the league."

"I am," I said. "I'm just going to Oxford first."

As we toured the US Capitol, meeting Rhodes Scholars who were members of Congress, Abdul told me how he wanted to make an equity-based run for governor in his home state of Michigan. Shad told how he wanted to bring Rhodes Scholarships to historically Black colleges and universities (HBCUs) in Mississippi. I thought, "I've found my people."

Two days later, my flight to London left from Ronald Reagan Washington National Airport. As I walked down the aisle with my bags, I saw a young woman wearing a white hijab and a warm smile. Her composure struck me—she was still without trying to be. My assigned seat was across from hers, and we struck up a conversation. She was also a Rhodes Scholar.

"Myron Rolle," I said, introducing myself.

"Aisha Saad," she said. "Our last names are next to each other in the alphabet. That's why we're seated together."

Aisha and I are both immigrants. When she was six, her family emigrated from Egypt to North Carolina. She went to UNC–Chapel Hill and is fluent in Spanish, English, and Arabic. "I can also read French and speak a bit of Hindi," she told me.

"Do you have brothers?" I asked, sensing a tough streak in her.

"I've got three brothers," Aisha replied. "I have to keep them in line."

"I've got four brothers," I said. "But I'm the baby."

"Family of athletes. Am I right?"

"I played football at FSU," I said. "I was supposed to be at the NFL draft right now, but I decided to go to Oxford. ESPN can't wrap their head around it."

"I understand," she replied. "I love sports, and I find beauty in people who balance athletics and school. I'm impressed you played football at a major school while still making time for the scholar inside yourself."

"What's impressive is that you speak five languages."

What drew me to Aisha was her openness about her faith. When she talked about Islam, her whole face lit up like she was describing the birth of a child. We had been talking nonstop for over two hours when she abruptly stopped the conversation. "I have to pray now," she explained.

"How will you be able to face Mecca?" I asked.

"Muslims always face forward on a plane when we pray. He knows where you are in the sky."

That struck me as profound. "Can I pray too?" I asked.

"You don't have to ask me to pray."

We faced forward, bent over, and offered ourselves in prayer. I said my Christian prayers while she said her Muslim ones. Though we had different faiths, I respected the depth and dedication of hers.

Aisha had a sense of humor. When our fellow Rhodes Scholars

came down the aisle to use the bathroom, we stuck out our arms to block them. "You have to pay the toll if you want to use the loo," she said, laughing.

We'd lift our arms only if they gave us a little shimmy. Over the course of the flight, the dances we required became more elaborate—we nearly had a mathematics major from MIT standing on his head.

By the time the plane landed at Heathrow, Aisha and I had prayed twice more. It felt natural, something familiar to take with me into a strange land. I stepped out of the airport into London's honking traffic with a renewed sense of purpose. Oxford was calling our names.

• • •

Oxford is a place ruled by knowledge. Because it was one of the only centers for learning in the Middle Ages, tensions often simmered between the feudal government and the university. In 1355, on Saint Scholastica Day, named for the saint of books and reading, students revolted against the mayor, rallying to the Church of St. Mary the Virgin. Battles raged for three days, and sixty-three students died in the fighting. The university prevailed, imprisoning the mayor and cementing a seat of power that has championed learning for eight hundred years.

On my first day in town, I climbed one hundred twenty-seven stairs to the roof of St. Mary's. Looking down High Street, I could see the shoe-worn steps of the Bodleian Library—an institution tasked with protecting millions of books—and many of Oxford's thirty-nine colleges. Academic honor and integrity seeped through their honey-colored stone.

My college, St. Edmund Hall, known to all as Teddy Hall, was tucked away at the southern end of a cobblestone alley called the Queen's Lane. Three-story medieval buildings looked out over a lopsided, green-grass quad where students milled about, sitting on the edge of the fountain, smoking cigarettes, and talking politics.

On move-in day, I lugged my bags through Teddy Hall's stone tunnel entrance, just as students had done for the last eight hundred years. Oxford is the world's oldest English-speaking university, and Teddy Hall is the oldest college at Oxford, estimated to be founded in 1236. Because it's affectionately known as the "jock" college, many of the young men on my floor were world-class rugby players.

Up a narrow, groaning staircase, I found a room with the white-washed walls and the woody smell of a country cottage. I unpacked, hanging my navy and black suits in the closet and stacking medical anthropology textbooks on a desk beneath the room's largest window. When I looked out through that window, I saw the Church of St. Peter-in-the-East, gray and Gothic, its sundial marking time.

Time meant something here. "Over centuries, thousands of students have performed the same move-in ritual in this room," I thought. "How many of them went on to change the world? Take your place in that history." I arranged my football gear into a neat pile that resembled a shrine, a reminder to keep my body in NFL shape. I had just finished refolding my parachute into a tight ball when a group of rugby players knocked on my door, asking if I wanted to go to a "presser" at the graveyard behind Teddy Hall's chapel. "It's tradition," they said. "Everyone drinks in the cemetery at night."

I told them I'd catch them next time, though I knew I wouldn't spend my nights howling at the moon over gravestones. I had to be up at five o'clock.

The sun hadn't had a chance to burn off the clouds encircling St. Peter-in-the-East's square tower when Cory pulled up the next morning in a green Peugeot. He lived in an apartment five minutes away; he would pick me up at Teddy Hall every morning at five thirty sharp. I folded myself into the tiny car, and we rumbled away down the cobblestone of Queen's Lane.

A light rain tapped the ground as we headed for Iffley Road Sports Centre. Cory wanted our first workout to take place where Roger Bannister became the first human to break the four-minute mile. Mist hung knee-high over the red rubber track. I bounced lightly on the soles of my shoes, warming up my muscles, feeling the history that had been run into this ground. Then I burst into a series of forty-yard sprints.

Each time I passed my brother, he urged me to verbalize my dreams. "In the first round of the 2010 NFL Draft, the New England Patriots select Myron Rolle, safety, Rhodes Scholar," I shouted with what little breath I had.

"Thirty-two Rhodes scholars, thirty-two first-rounders," Cory said. "What are you going to be?"

"Thirty-two, thirty-two."

"What's that?"

"Thirty-two, thirty-two!"

When I finished, I squatted on the grass, lungs heaving. The sun had begun its feeble assault against the dreary sky, and the sweat was indistinguishable from the morning dew on my skin.

Cory threw me a protein shake and took a knee next to me. "It doesn't matter if we're on this historical track or knee-deep in mud on a soggy rugby pitch," he said. "I'm going to be there in that tiny car with this protein shake every morning, and we're going to get it."

I hugged my brother, and we stood and walked back toward the Peugeot together as the church bells tolled the eight o'clock hour.

Later that morning, I put on my suit, knotting my tie in a full Windsor, and joined the throngs of students heading to class. As I walked among them, I wasn't conscious of my skin color in the same way I had been in the States. I wasn't the Black kid dressing up in a suit and tie to blend in with the white preps. I was a scholar honoring the traditions of the hallowed halls of the oldest English-speaking university on earth.

I was passing beneath the seventeen stone heads of the bearded men who sat atop the gate of Oxford's Sheldonian Theatre, in which music and lectures had echoed since 1669, when I spotted Aisha and waved her over.

"Myron," she said, coming up to me excitedly. "My college is *the* place where they filmed Harry Potter. I feel like Hermione Granger."

"This place is too dope. Look," I said, pointing to the Sheldonian's upcoming schedule. "Sandra Day O'Connor is speaking here next month."

"We'll go together," Aisha said. "I just want to soak it all in."

"Let's have breakfast on Friday," I said. "We can review our first week."

"See you then; now get to class."

My graduate studies were focused on medical anthropology, which uses social, cultural, biological, and linguistic anthropology to better understand health and well-being. The field tries to understand how the cultural importance of medical systems relates to the prevention and treatment of sickness and healing processes. My cohort consisted of twelve students from all over the world. My first week, I connected with a young woman from Canada named Hayden Lindsey, and Jerry Aguiar, a Rhodes Scholar from California.

I think the three of us knew we would need one another. Our professors let us know from day one that they expected us to meet Oxford's unparalleled academic standards. It wasn't enough to speak or write eloquently—precise medical and scientific terminology had to be used in the proper context; deep research had to back every assertion; meaning was to be found in nuance, not black-and-white declarations; and vague words like *metaphysical* were challenged, revealed to be hollow. Professors had no qualms about reducing your ideas to rubble with a linguistic wrecking ball.

At the end of the first week, I met with one of my professors to go over a proposal for a paper defending ritualistic healing in Burkina Faso. He eviscerated my work, berating me with a vigor that would have made Coach Andrews proud, albeit with less spittle and profanity. Most of my papers at Florida State had easily earned top marks, so it was tough to stomach his verbal beating.

After he had finished his systematic destruction of my proposal, my professor did something that surprised me. "Good job, Myron," he told me. "Come back next week, and we'll do it again."

I was confused. Why would he praise me after telling me off for being an awful writer for the last hour? Then I realized that Coach Andrews had done the same thing. My professor criticized my work because he was invested in my improvement.

Still, the measure by which I had missed the mark left me demoralized. I questioned whether I had picked the wrong field of study. When Aisha spoke about her courses over proper English fry-ups in a café in downtown Oxford destined to become our regular haunt, she seemed more settled in her field. She planned to analyze how fragmentation in international environmental law shaped legal structures that protect equitable development, and her poised, informed confidence amazed me. When I shared my doubts with her, she nodded knowingly.

"Don't be afraid to reach out," she said. "You have Oxford at your fingertips. Use it."

"I'll talk to some of my classmates," I said. "One of them is a Rhodes." I waved down the waitress. "Can I get another one of these?" I asked, pointing to my plate, which I had just relieved of two eggs, bacon, sausage, thick-cut ham, and beans.

"How do you eat so much?" Aisha asked, amused.

"Wind sprints at 5:30 a.m. make you hungry. You should have seen the damage the football team did to the breakfast buffet at Florida State."

"I shudder to think," Aisha said. "You know, I have doubts too. Maybe not in the classroom, but I wonder what my future looks like. I'm a Muslim woman. How do I handle going into higher education while keeping the standards of my faith? What does a career in English academia look like for a woman like me?"

"That's something I worry about in America," I said.

"All the way up the ladder, no matter how high we climb, we'll have to navigate carefully," Aisha said. "Our stories will look different than most."

"Faith will guide me," I said. "I may not always have confidence in the classroom, but I'm confident in that."

"Above all else," Aisha said, nodding.

"I think about my parents," I said. "Even over here, I can hear my daddy's voice. I listen to him."

"Ah," Aisha said, smirking at me. "Here's your second breakfast."

Before we left for campus, we prayed together, each of us speaking the words of our respective faiths.

When we neared Teddy Hall, Aisha and I passed the cemetery behind St. Peter-in-the-East, where students skulled beer at night. Aisha, who had been telling me about her mother's Egyptian food, stopped talking, put her head down, and continued to walk. I worried I had said something to offend her. Once we had passed the graveyard, she lifted her head and resumed talking about how much she missed her family's *koshari*.

"What was that?" I asked.

"In Islam, when you pass a graveyard, you show respect to the dead," she told me.

"I respect that," I said. "I'm going to take that up, if you don't mind."

"You be accountable to God the best way you see fit," Aisha replied, steady but smiling.

Her discipline made me think about my Christian walk. Did I need to be more accountable? I didn't drink or smoke, but I still had sinful thoughts and fell short of the glory of God. What if I applied to my faith the seriousness with which Aisha approached hers? How could I use the 2% Way to help me get closer to God by learning lessons from a Muslim's faith in God? From that day onward, every time I passed that cemetery, which was nearly every day on the way to class, I bowed my head. It reminded me to keep my promises to God. If I did that, the rest was in his hands.

I still had to retool my paper—a first draft was due in a week. "They are going to destroy your work again," I thought. "It will be embarrassing." I cut that mental dialogue off at the knees by reinjecting the 2% Way into my thought process. "You might not write the best paper," I told myself, "but you can make small improvements on your last one." Progress, not perfection: a tough sell at Oxford, but a leap I had to make.

I called on my classmates to help me to inch my way forward. Hayden Lindsey, Jerry Aguiar, and I formed a study group. We shared physician articles, picking apart how medical anthropologists spoke and the buzzwords they used. By reaching out, I had taken the first step toward improvement, 2 percent at a time.

Through this study group, I realized I needed to redefine my research topic. I switched course, diving deep into epigenetic studies of indigenous hunter-gatherers in the Americas. They had developed a specific gene that enabled them to store extra fat in their bellies. This allowed them to survive leaner months or seasons, and those who survived passed down their genetic trait to their offspring. Known as the thrifty gene theory, what once was an evolutionary advantage has now become a modern-day liability. Many Native American ancestors who have the gene now suffer from obesity, hypertension, and diabetes. In an era in which food is plentiful, this genetic mutation is now an evolutionary disadvantage. This topic had legs—I could plumb its depths and conduct original research. If I put in the time, I would have a solid foundation to build on over the coming weeks.

I spent hours writing at my dormitory desk that looked out at St. Peter-in-the-East's sundial, its shadow slowly marking the hours. *Put in the time.* I'd never committed that much effort to a single paper, and when I handed it to my professor, I knew I had done all I could do.

"I'll see you on Monday, Mr. Rolle," he said. "We will discuss your work."

That night was our first formal dinner. We had to wear an outfit of capes and tuxes with white bow ties called a "sub fusc." I sat between Shad, who went to St. John's, the alma mater of former British prime minister Tony Blair, and Abdul, who attended Oriel College, where Cecil Rhodes himself once studied. Everyone at the table seemed natural in this incredibly formal setting. "Hey, did you hear about the genocide that's going on in Kuala Lumpur?" someone asked the table.

"Rohingya people have faced persecution for a long time," Abdul replied. "This is just the most recent explosion of violence."

I quickly realized the dialogues at Oxford would be far beyond the scope of the talk around the dinner table at my athletic suite on Tennessee Street in Florida. No offense to my boys at FSU, but if it wasn't girls, music, or spades, we were talking about the NFL. Here I realized I needed to be ready to have cerebral interactions any time, day or night. Shad, Abdul, and the rest of the Rhodes Scholars talked all evening about Gaddafi, the United Nations and the G8 Summit, and Barack Obama and the Nobel Prize.

These complex conversations brought up insecurities about being "just a jock," insecurities that ran from the depths of my gray matter to my frontal lobe and the most active synapses in my white matter. I wanted my peers to know I was there to learn and to believe I was there on equal footing.

For the rest of the evening, I was quieter than usual. When someone asked the table, "Hey, did you hear about the new policy paper on climate change presented to the UN?" I didn't speak up because, frankly, I hadn't.

When I got back to Teddy Hall that night, I turned on the BBC. Prime Minister David Cameron was giving an interview about issues with the National Health Service. I sat down and watched, noting where I agreed or disagreed with his policies. The next morning, as

Cory and I drove back from our predawn workout, I asked him to stop the car at a magazine stand, where I bought a copy of *The Times*.

"More reading?" he asked.

"Let's learn about the Arab Spring in Phoenicia," I said, scanning the headlines.

"Tell me all about it," Cory said.

At the next formal dinner, I was prepared to talk about any subject that might arise. But that night nobody was talking about the Arab Spring. Dave Hille, an Aussie who had become a close friend, was leading an expedition to Málaga, Spain. The group planned to leave the next morning and spend the weekend party-hopping down the Costa del Sol, a coastal stretch along Andalusia's southeastern coast lined with stunning beaches.

"Come with us, Myron," Dave said. "We'll go swimming in the Alboran Sea at midnight."

"I've never been to the beach in Spain," I thought. I remembered Bill Bradley's advice to see other countries. Why not? I might never have the opportunity again. "I'll think about it," I said.

The next morning at five thirty, I heard the familiar *tut-tut* of the Peugeot. Today, since Channel 4 hadn't called for rain, we'd work out on the best grass field available: an elderly Englishman's yard. I imagine the first time we showed up there, he was shocked to see two Black men exercising at the crack of dawn—and probably too nervous to say anything.

Cory parked and handed me my protein shake. "Let's go get it."

"Always do."

Cory grabbed four cones from the Peugeot's back seat and set them up into a ten-yard by ten-yard square. I got into position, backpedaled to a parallel cone, shuffled to the next one, sprinted, shuffled. Repeat, repeat, repeat. These were the same drills Cory and I had done with Daddy as boys on the sand in Atlantic City—my muscles remembered everything.

"What are you going to be?" Cory asked.

"Thirty-two." Sprint. "Thirty-two." Shuffle. "The first ever," I called out into the morning.

It turns out, if you do enough conditioning drills, you can burn the thought of Málaga from your mind.

On Monday, the Málaga group returned with tales of late nights in the city that had birthed Picasso. "We were like characters from an expatriate novel," Dave Hille told me. "*Heaps* of fun."

"Glad you had a good time," I said, distracted. My mind was on other things: I had to meet with my professor about my paper draft that afternoon. I was mentally preparing for another excoriation.

My professor complimented my topic and my depth of research but attacked my writing itself. My language was imprecise, and I repeated phrases far too often. "We must use the right word, not its second cousin," he said. "Mark Twain said that. An American."

I took the paper from him and looked over the litany of red circles covering the page.

"Good work," he said. "Next week, I trust you'll have something new to show me."

I needed tools that would chip away at the deficits in my prose. My professor had said that my writing didn't follow the form of a medical anthropologist. "How do I link ideas together like a medical anthropologist?" I wondered.

Too often in my writing, I used medical terms like *obesogenic*. I dropped them into my papers as crutches, not always using them correctly and appropriately, which prevented me from articulating more detailed thoughts. By eliminating overused words, I made my papers 2 percent better by unlocking more contextual thinking. Using precise vocabulary allowed me to think about things from a different dimension, with nuance and expertise replacing simpler, less distinct concepts.

The resulting paper earned me my first A at Oxford, and the research became the subject of my Oxford thesis. I would bring this knowledge back to help the Seminole Tribe of Florida when I returned to the States. Coach Andrews's 2% Way had made its mark on English academia, something a South Alabama football coach probably never expected.

As soon as I received my marks, I texted Aisha: "A on the paper! I think I've found my thesis subject."

"God is good!" she replied. "Tell me all about it at breakfast Friday."

As my days went on, I applied the 2 percent process to keeping myself informed. I read the London *Times* every day and continued to stay abreast of world events by watching Sky News and listening to BBC Radio. I knew I could hold court with the best and brightest. I had moved past my insecurity to a place where I was excited to engage in complex discussions because I had prepared for them.

"What are your thoughts on our benefactor, Cecil Rhodes?" Shad asked the table one night at a formal dinner.

"He's an example of how respect for native cultures must be at the forefront of our mind when we're doing outreach in the developing world," I said.

"How so?"

"He was someone who wanted to go out and change the world. But his colonial views, his racism, didn't allow him to respect the people he was trying to help. Postcolonialism has shaped how I think about global health. Someday, when I operate in Africa or the Caribbean, I'm going to make sure I understand and respect religious practices, family structures, and medical traditions. Western medicine should be in conversation with a region's history, not seek to erase it."

"I'll drink to that," Shad said, raising his beer.

I clinked my cranberry juice against his Guinness bottle.

● ● ●

Though they eventually accepted my academic seriousness, my British professors cocked their eyebrows at my NFL aspirations.

Most of them had never watched a single snap of the sport, let alone played one. Their myopia didn't let them see value beyond academia. The irony of the similarities to the sports world wasn't lost on me.

I refused to be myopic. Instead, I let Oxford open my world. I immersed myself in campus life, taking classes on topics I had never heard of. I did a study on the French philosopher René Descartes, learning how the senses are not meant to provide knowledge of the "essential nature" of inanimate objects, but that innate ideas govern this nature, independent of any sensory image. I took that to mean that God and the soul breathed through everything. I took to the rugby pitch quite a few times and knocked some English blokes around. I went to lectures at the Sheldonian Theatre—my favorite was Sandra Day O'Connor, the first female Supreme Court justice. She talked about how, after spending her childhood on the Lazy B, her family's ranch in Arizona, her parents sent her to live with her grandmother in El Paso to give her the best chance at a quality education. She thrived at the Radford School for Girls and graduated high school two years early. "I can relate to that," I thought. "I've motored through every school I've ever been to."

I grew socially and intellectually 2 percent at a time. I would go to bars with Shad, where he drank beer, and I drank cranberry juice. After last call, Shad and I would sit on his doorstep at three in the morning, talking about our plans to bring more HBCU students into the Rhodes program. Shad was particularly passionate about this subject and would talk until daylight if I let him.

My friendship with Aisha continued to grow, expanding beyond our Friday breakfasts. We ate many of our meals together, either at Teddy Hall or her college, Christ Church, which really did feel like you were stepping into Hogwarts. It was refreshing to speak to somebody on the same wavelength as I was on almost every subject, from family and music to sports. We could be totally open with each other.

"Can I tell you something?" she asked one day as we walked down High Street on a Sunday afternoon, looking at the sausage rolls and Cornish pasties stacked in the windows of the bakeries.

"You can tell me anything," I replied.

"You're my best friend at Oxford," she said. "I think I knew it was meant to be that day when you got down to pray with me on the plane. You weren't some jock chatting me up. I saw you as someone serious about getting to know my culture, my faith."

Instinctively, I reached out to hug her. I'm a hugger—have been since I was a kid—and always embrace people I love. But Aisha moved away from my embrace.

"Did I do something wrong?" I asked.

"Muslim women can't touch anyone but their husband in that way," she said.

"I'm embarrassed."

"Don't worry. I've had this conversation with a lot of people," Aisha said. "We'll settle for a fist bump."

"Just like with my homeboys," I said, dabbing her up.

I appreciated the way Aisha drew that line in the sand. As we walked, she explained that even though the hug was innocent and based on friendship, it still violated a promise she had made to God. That's the sign of a strong friendship—someone who continues to teach you as you grow together.

"This doesn't mean we can't have fun together," Aisha said. "You've got your thesis all wrapped up. Let's do something spontaneous."

I remembered Bill Bradley's advice to let experience drive me. "After formal dinner tonight, let's have a bit of fun," I said.

That night, after debating the politics of Croatia over black pudding, Aisha and I stole away from the crowd. Still dressed in our sub fuscs, we took photos at all our favorite spots on campus. She snapped one of me grinning in front of Teddy Hall; I took a picture of her looking at the Sheldonian Theatre. As I stuck my arms out to form a Heisman pose in front of the library, one of our professors walked by, shaking his head. I flexed even harder, and Aisha and I collapsed into a fit of laughter.

● ● ●

In December 2009, I came back from a day of Christmas shopping in London with Cory and saw a letter peeking out of my mailbox at Teddy Hall. One of my FSU professors had sent me a recently published *Wall Street Journal* article titled "Can Scholars Make Dollars in the NFL?" "Some scouts already view Mr. Rolle's delay as a sign that he's not serious about becoming an elite player and doubt if he is training well enough in England," the piece said. "And since he isn't playing, some companies have hesitated to sign him."[2]

My whole life's plan was predicated on the proposition that I could be both a Rhodes Scholar and an elite NFL player. It seemed not everyone agreed. I called Cory. "Come over and bring the gear," I said. "I got something to show you."

Cory pulled up in the Peugeot, and I handed him the article. He read it, his face deepening into a frown, and then ripped it in half.

"You know where we're going, right?" I asked.

"Get in," he said. "I made two protein shakes today."

We drove back to Iffley Sports Centre, where we had worked out my first day at Oxford. I'd never sprinted so hard in my life—I sweated like I was back in Tallahassee in August doing up-downs to the cruel sound of Coach Andrews's whistle. During mornings of training with Cory, I built my body into game shape the 2% Way. I did heavy lifts, then went out onto the rugby pitch and drilled with my weight vest, parachute, and ankle weights.

If I wanted to be one of the top thirty-two players selected in the draft, I would need to keep improving the 2% Way mentally as well as physically. I called up Coach Andrews and had him send me game tape. I studied the video as closely as I had my medical anthropology textbooks and analyzed packages over Skype with Andrews. He walked me through offensive schemes they might run in the NFL, letting me know what to watch for and how to react. I watched NFL football on Mondays, Sundays, and Thursdays and college football on Saturdays to stay mentally sharp and connected to the game I had been away from for a year. I was determined to prove everyone wrong about getting into the league. The NFL Combine was in February, only a few months away. When I stepped onto the field, I would be ready.

I remain close with Shad White, Abdul El-Sayed, and Dave Hille to this day. They are all changing the world in ways that we dreamed of on Oxford's campus. Abdul made that run for governor of Michigan, and now he's a political commentator. When I turn on CNN and see him arguing about equity, I smile because I know he's still got that fire. Shad is now the auditor for the state of Mississippi and is eventually going to be governor one day. We're working together on a joint program to try to bring Rhodes Scholarships to HBCUs in Mississippi and other states, just as we talked about on those late nights on the steps of Teddy Hall.

Aisha is still one of my best friends. Married with a young daughter, she lives near me in Boston, where she works as a fellow at the Forum on Corporate Governance at Harvard Law School. She has clerked for US district attorneys and has published widely on sustainable fundraising. She's grown into the leader she dreamed of becoming as we wandered around Oxford's campus together.

Taking the Rhodes was the best decision I've ever made. But like all decisions, foregoing the draft for Oxford came with consequences, consequences I would have to face as soon as I set back down on American soil.

Chapter 6

WITH THE 207TH PICK . . .

School was out: I was now in the football *business*. The NFL is an entirely different animal than the college game. I needed people on my team who had expertise wrangling the cagiest parts of that animal. As soon as my feet touched American soil, I hired Leigh Steinberg, the sports agent who had been the inspiration for Tom Cruise's character in *Jerry Maguire*.

Steinberg had brokered monster deals for Ben Roethlisberger, John Elway, and Troy Aikman. He'd represented the No. 1 pick in the NFL draft a record eight times, most famously guiding the early days of Steve Young's career. If anyone could get my name back in the mix, it was Steinberg.

Cory and I flew to Steinberg's sparkling office in Newport Beach, California. My new agent told me that he too was an outsider trying to get back into the upper echelons of the sports world. He'd taken risks, faced down some demons, but had battled back to the top.

"You're saying the NFL views me as an outsider?" I asked.

"I'll put it this way," Steinberg said. "I'm aware of what they're writing about you in the press. I hear things in NFL insider circles. Some teams keep questioning your commitment. They think you abandoned your teammates in college."

A false narrative with a real impact. I couldn't erase that damage. I *could* destroy unfounded perceptions through my play. I had an uphill climb ahead of me if I was to hear my name called in the first round. I would have to grab 2 percent from every moment from now until draft day.

"Let's smash that story and tell a new one," I said to Steinberg.

"What's that story going to be?" he asked, tenting his hands on a gleaming desk.

"Myron Rolle is back like he never left."

First step: The Senior Bowl. On January 30, the best seniors in the nation would descend on Ladd-Peebles Stadium in Mobile, Alabama, to prove themselves one last time as student-athletes. The North faces off against the South in a game with BCS Bowl intensity and Pro Bowl talent. The game would be my reintroduction to the NFL—general managers and head coaches from every single team would have their eyes trained on the field. It was the ideal venue to showcase that I could still compete at the highest level. If I played well, I'd earn an invite to the NFL Combine.

On the first day of the Senior Bowl, every player had to walk onstage at the stadium's amphitheater to be weighed and measured wearing nothing but a pair of spandex. The announcer called, "Myron Rolle, Florida State, safety," and I stepped onstage, hearing rumblings, murmurs. The scouts were gabbing, but I kept my eyes trained dead ahead and stepped onto the scale: 217, my fighting weight. I silently thanked Cory for pulling up in the Peugeot every morning in England.

The following day, I went online to check on those rumblings. The first article I saw talked about how GMs were saying I was the showstopper of the day. "Thank goodness I stayed away from those fish and chips at Oxford," I thought. So far, so good. Time to attack practice.

The depth chart listed me as the third-string safety. That was fair—I hadn't played in eighteen months. A familiar chip re-formed on my shoulder. I wouldn't let myself be third string when the whistle blew at the Senior Bowl's kickoff. "How can I improve by two percent every single day?" I asked myself in the hotel room that night. "How can I get to a point where I can play more snaps on Saturday when important eyes are looking in my direction?"

The Miami Dolphins staff coached my team, the South. I knew Miami ran a hard-nosed defense that valued hustle. I could stand out to their defensive coordinators by injecting ferocity into my game, the same intensity that had made me an All-American at FSU. The first couple of days of practice, I locked down Tim Tebow's top receiver from the University of Florida, Riley Cooper. I dominated Cooper, covering him like a glove during one-on-ones. I shut down every other receiver I lined up against, knocking them off their feet. I blew up play after play.

The Detroit Lions staff coached the North team. After I batted down a slant pass, their defensive coordinator called to me from the opposing sideline. "Rolle, I love the way you're playing. So physical out there. I didn't know you still had it in you."

I thanked him but wished he hadn't added that last part. More fuel for my 2 percent flame. I would switch the narrative from "We're surprised he's back" to "Why did we think he ever left?"

The depth chart reflected my hustle. On day two I moved up from the third team to the second unit. By the fourth day, I had been promoted to first string. In December I'd been ankle-deep in mud on a rugby pitch in Oxford; in January I started in the 2010 Senior Bowl. That's the tremendous impact of the 2% Way.

When I went out on the field on game day, I felt like I was home. Toward the end of the game, our backs were against the goal line. The North tried to punch it into the end zone with an off-tackle lead drive. I followed behind our linebacker—he smashed into their fullback, and I hurled myself into the running back. I stonewalled him for a loss of two yards.

The North won by a few touchdowns, but I got in my snaps.

After the game, a reporter from Fox Sports approached me. "What's it like playing football again?" he asked. For the first time in eighteen months, a journalist hadn't brought up Oxford. I was finally back to Xs and Os.

"I like being yelled at," I replied, happy to be answering football questions again. "I like the pads popping. I like the smell of the grass."

The next day, the *Sun Sentinel* ran a piece with the headline "Myron Rolle a Hit at Senior Bowl." The reporter quoted an NFL scout. "He's looking great," the scout said. "For a guy who hasn't played in a while, he's done everything you'd want. He's making people notice him. No one really came here thinking about him, and he's jumped out a little."[1]

On the last day of the Senior Bowl, NFL teams reached out for initial interviews. Each time Cory's phone rang with news from Steinberg, I felt validated. I met with Matt Patricia, the defensive coordinator of the New England Patriots, my dream NFL destination. Next up were the Pittsburgh Steelers and the Jacksonville Jaguars. My most promising meeting was with the Tampa Bay Buccaneers. "They are *very* interested," Steinberg told me.

I met with head coach Raheem Morris, their general manager, their assistant coach, and their top scouts. "I told my son that you went to Oxford," Morris said as we settled into our chairs in a conference room. "You're a role model for my boy."

But the NFL is not in the business of role models. The Bucs personnel flipped the script and started to grill me. "How do you think your teammates felt when you abandoned them and went to England?" they asked.

"They were appreciative that I was able to have the opportunity to study at Oxford," I replied, trying to remain calm. "They supported it." I told them about how my Seminole family had linked hands and prayed for me the day before my Rhodes interview.

The scouts frowned, scribbling on their yellow legal pads. The uncomfortable questions continued. "But how would you feel if the best player on the team left while he still had a year of eligibility remaining?" asked a guy in an Under Armour polo. "Weren't your teammates counting on you?"

"Ask *them* if I let them down," I said. "They know the truth."

Coach Morris stepped in, sensing the agitation in my curt answer. "Myron, let's talk football."

"I'd love to," I replied. "You guys like to run a Cover Two Sink. My size works well in that scheme."

I talked Xs and Os for another twenty minutes, but something was amiss. I couldn't understand how this question about whether I was committed to football or to my academics was coming up again after I'd just proven myself on the field. Their insistence on pushing the narrative that I wasn't committed to football sowed a seed of discontent in my mind. I thought, "This is going to be my downfall in the NFL. I'm never going to get a fair shot to play this sport to my utmost. Teams think I've simply been eating bangers and mash, listening to Sandra Day O'Connor, and punting on the Thames."

My performance at the Senior Bowl earned me an invitation to the NFL Combine held in March in Indianapolis, Indiana. From the moment I walked into the lobby of the hotel that the NFL had taken over in downtown Indianapolis, you could cut the tension with a knife. All the top talent strutted by, sizing each other up. I saw Andre Smith, a lineman from Alabama, eyeballing Tim Tebow.

The NFL Combine was the most stressful week of my life. It consisted of several days of interviews, physical performances, and mind games that the general managers, coaches, and scouts play. We players had to walk out in our underwear while medical teams examined our bodies for signs of injury or imperfection. It made me feel like human cattle. We didn't get much sleep over the few days there, waking each morning at four o'clock, but they expected us to perform at the highest level.

In the combine, a defensive back's forty-yard dash time will make or break him in an instant. That day, beset by lack of sleep and shot nerves, I ran a 4.59. It wasn't Deion Sanders fast (4.27), but it was only 2/100ths of a second slower than Ed Reed, who was one of the best safeties ever to play the game. But it still wasn't indicative of my speed. I typically ran a 4.4.

I resolved to do better in the physical drills that followed, but I never felt fluid. I placed extra pressure on myself to do every single movement perfectly, and as a result, none of them felt smooth. I didn't feel like I grabbed 2 percent from that week. I might have lost 2 percent due to the stress. I wondered if this might be the first real failure of my life.

Once the combine ended, I couldn't wait to get home to Orlando, where I had been living and training since I got back from England. I gave myself two days to lie in bed, something I had never done before. The combine was an opportunity that comes around only once in a lifetime, and I hadn't performed at the level I knew I was capable of. That was on me. I got in the way of myself and the 2% Way.

Because of my showing in Indianapolis, Steinberg and I decided to hold my own pro day, where I would rerun my forty-yard dash. In the weeks leading up to the event, I trained every day with Cory. I pushed myself physically and mentally: 2 percent smarter, 2 percent faster. I was determined to erase the impression I had made at the combine.

When Steinberg called up NFL scouts to invite them, many of them were dismissive. "He's going to be running alone," one of them said.

I didn't run alone. One team showed up to my pro day: the New York Giants. I improved my forty-meter time from 4.59 seconds to 4.48. "Not perfect, but I'll take it," I thought. The Giants scouts seemed engaged. They didn't bring up Oxford. I took that as a good sign—perhaps I would end up playing my NFL ball at the Meadowlands, only a few hours' drive from where I had first set foot on a football field.

• • •

The 2010 NFL Draft would be held at Radio City Music Hall on the evening of April 22 and would continue for three nights until Roger Goodell announced the 255th, and final, pick. Days ahead of time, hordes of reporters, celebrities, and face-painted fans swarmed the hotels lining Sixth Avenue. Analysts speculated into ESPN's cameras for hours of airtime, debating the futures of NFL hopefuls who came to New York dressed in their best suits—some tailored classics, some loud and splashy—praying to make good on a dream they'd chased since childhood.

Those dreams, and the stories behind them, are the reason why millions have watched draft night from home since the 1980s, when ESPN began their nationally televised broadcast. The first-round condenses all the pageantry, paychecks, and heartbreak of football into a single spectacle. Lives change in moments; cold realization dashes hopes. The undersized receiver from a small school unexpectedly goes in the top ten. A man who can bench press two hundred twenty-five pounds forty times sobs tears of joy in his father's arms. A running back who slept in his car as a kid can suddenly buy his mama a house. A top quarterback grimaces as he falls down the board, losing millions of dollars with every passing minute.

For the players, seconds feel like hours. Every name called that is not your own is another prick of disappointment, another layer of anxiety.

The day before draft night, I went to New York City to meet with Roger Goodell. His office had reached out to Cory, saying the commissioner wanted to talk to me because he was proud of what I stood for. Goodell introduced me to Pat Haden, the former Los Angeles Rams quarterback who had also been a Rhodes Scholar. The three of us talked about how the skills I had learned at Oxford would translate to the league.

"The NFL needs more players like you," Goodell told me when

I left. Goodell's vote of confidence lifted my spirits. If the man at the top wanted me in the league, perhaps my draft stock hadn't fallen as far as I feared.

That night, I went to *ESPN The Magazine*'s annual predraft party at a swanky venue called ESPACE in the Hell's Kitchen neighborhood of Manhattan. A sea of cameras blitzed hot prospects like Dez Bryant and Rob Gronkowski as they arrived dressed to the nines. I strutted down the red carpet and flashed my best smile to a constellation of flashbulbs. Inside, Alyssa Milano and Ice-T danced to DJ Questlove's tunes. Since we were in the Big Apple, New York Giants were in the house; I recognized Chris Canty, Gerris Wilkinson, Ramses Barden, and Hakeem Nicks. If all went well the next day, I might be their teammate.

I saw Adrian Peterson hanging with T.I., whose hit "Whatever You Like" blasted through the night. *Stacks on deck . . . Baby, you can have whatever you like.* The lyrics crystallized the energy in the room—young men at the precipice of having the world at their fingertips. I wasn't infatuated with the glitz or interested in a future of popping bottles in velvet-roped VIP areas, but I certainly felt the magnitude of what the next seventy-two hours would bring. We had worked our whole lives to be one of the chosen few who play on Sunday. Tomorrow we would know which of us would take the final step into that new, glittering world.

The next day, the Rolle family assembled at my house in Orlando. Marvis arrived first, wearing a megawatt grin and a collared polo shirt.

"Rahlu!" I exclaimed, hugging him tightly.

"No place in the world I'd rather be," he said. Rahlu has always been the kindest of the Rolles.

"Where's Whitney?" I asked.

"Five minutes behind me."

Rahlu, Whitney, Cory, and Myron watching ESPN together was just like the old days when we huddled around the family television set in Galloway. My eldest brother Marchant called us to big me up as Mummy set out trays of wings, rice, and macaroni and cheese. I grabbed a glass of *switcha*, which is Bahamian for lemonade. My fit was clean: Louis Vuitton leather shoes, matching brown pants, and a crisp Oxford.

Daddy watched over the party, pleased to have his boys under the same roof, trying not to show his nerves. Coverage kicked off at 7:30 p.m., the first time the draft had run in a prime-time programming slot. I was thankful for a few private hours with my family before the camera crews knocked on the door. The NFL Network and ESPN, who had run specials on my time at Oxford, were producing follow-up pieces chronicling "the Rhodes Scholar's journey to the league." I had grown accustomed to cameras and knew how to mask my emotions, but I'd never been this nervous in my life. When I faced challenges, I calmed myself through action by improving 2 percent at a clip. Now I had to sit back and wait for others to decide my fate.

Just before the film crews arrived, Cory pulled me aside. "No matter what happens, you earned your place in the league," he said. "All those early mornings in the rain, all the times you did what you needed to do instead of what was easy. It's time to take your place."

"Thirty-two, thirty-two."

"Thirty-two, thirty-two."

I heard Daddy open the door. "Come in, come in," he said. "We've got food if you're hungry. Myron! ESPN is here."

Showtime.

"It's on!" Mummy called from the couch. I beelined past the food—one of the only times in my life I haven't had an appetite—and took my place next to my mother. It was time.

The broadcast opened with Jay-Z's "Empire State of Mind" booming over shots of the Empire State Building and yellow cabs racing down Broadway. "Welcome to the city of dreams. Welcome to the club," a narrator announced. "Tomorrow's NFL stars take their place on football's brightest stage to see their dreams realized and their destinies unfold." Mummy clasped my hand, her grip as tight as her embrace had been after I had won the Rhodes.

The St. Louis Rams were up first and, as expected, took quarterback Sam Bradford. Bradford had won the Heisman the previous year, leading his Sooners to the highest-scoring offense in NCAA history. Had I accepted the scholarship Bob Stoops had offered me in high school, I might have been his teammate. Bradford donned a white Rams hat, strutted to the stage, and posed with his new jersey and Goodell.

Picks fell off the board every ten minutes. I paid close attention to my position—safety—as that might give me a better indication of where I stood. Our class was chock-full of talented safeties. The first to go was Eric Berry at five to Kansas City. Then the Seattle Seahawks picked Earl Thomas at fourteen.

"The Giants pick next," Rahlu said.

I steeled my nerves—this was my best chance to go in the first round. Goodell looked down at the cue card and began to read. "With the fifteenth pick in the 2010 NFL Draft, the New York Giants select . . ."

I breathed deep. *Thirty-two, thirty-two. This is it. Take your place in history.*

"Jason Pierre-Paul, linebacker, University of South Florida."

I let go of Mummy's hand. Thankfully, she held on to mine. Dread entered my veins; my heart seemed to slow and quicken at the same time. A second later, my phone rang. A spark of hope sprang into my heart—every prospect knows to answer their phone on the first ring on draft day. It's usually good news. I jumped to my feet and answered an unknown number with a 212 area code.

"Myron," said a voice I faintly recognized. "This is Chris Mara from the New York Giants."

"Oh, hello, sir," I replied, slightly confused. The Giants weren't up again until the second round.

"I want to tell you you're a great player, and you're a great young man. We'd be lucky to have you. But we've decided to go in a different direction this year."

"You needed a linebacker," I said. "I understand."

"That's right," he said. "You take care, son. We aren't worried about you."

I hung up the phone. Mummy looked up at me, her eyes trying to communicate some measure of comfort. Maybe the Giants weren't worried about my future, but I was starting to.

"I'm not going to be a Giant," I announced to the room.

"It's all good," Cory said. "The Patriots are at twenty-seven. You always wanted to play in that defense."

I sat back down next to Mummy and waited. And waited. Tim Tebow went to the Denver Broncos with the twenty-fifth pick, shocking the sports world. The Patriots pick came and went. Still I waited.

After three hours and twenty-eight minutes, the Saints took Patrick Robinson, a cornerback and my teammate at Florida State, with the last pick of the first round. I was happy for my fellow Seminole, but a heaviness descended on me as though someone had turned my blood to lead. The sound from the television seemed far away, almost as if it were playing from behind a closed door.

Mummy let go of my hand and stood up, a look of disappointment etched across her face. Her eyes scanned the room, searching for something, anything, to busy herself with. Slowly, she packed up the catered food. "Nobody touched the wings," she said in a soft voice as she wrapped them in tinfoil and stacked the trays.

When Daddy saw Mummy stop and stare at the refrigerator before opening it, a tray of uneaten food in her hands, he exploded. "They're punishing you, Myron," he said, his deep voice rising in anger. "They're punishing you."

Throughout the evening, each member of the Rolle family had felt that sentiment. We knew it deep in our souls. But we had not verbalized it in the hope that we might be wrong.

"This is not right. This is not right," Daddy said, pacing the room. The cameramen trained their lenses on his moving figure. One of the production assistants pushed his boom mic in my father's direction.

"Daddy," I said. "I know you're upset, but goodness gracious, please. Don't kill the—"

"No, no, no. This is wrong. Let them film me. You did everything they asked you to do. They're punishing you because you went to Oxford. They are punishing you for your intelligence."

"Yes, Daddy," I said. "I know."

"We still have tomorrow," said Rahlu. "Samari was a second-round pick. He balled out for ten seasons."

"We expected that you might go in the second or third round," Cory said. "We were prepared for this."

True, I had prepared myself for the probable reality of dropping to the second or third round, but I knew I should have gone earlier. If I hadn't taken the Rhodes, Commissioner Goodell would have called my name that night, and I would have hugged Mummy and mugged for the cameras. I would have achieved the dream I had committed myself to for more than a decade. All that evaporated in just over three hours.

Before Daddy snapped off the television, I heard Scott Van Pelt say that 7.29 million people watched the first round, the most viewed draft in television history at that point.

Lying in bed that night, I heard Daddy's footsteps wearing out the rug in the hallway. "It's all right, Whitney," said Mummy's voice. "It's all right."

"No," Daddy said. "No, it's not."

● ● ●

A bright beam of Florida sunlight streaming through my curtains woke me the following morning. It took my brain a moment to reload the events of the last twenty-four hours. My new reality slowly sank in. But once it had, I decided to approach day two with optimism. I still had a good chance of going in the second or third round. I could work with that. I made sure I fully charged my phone. *Today it will ring with good news*, I told myself.

My brothers and I tore into the previous night's leftovers. "Told you they wouldn't go to waste," Whitney told Mummy. Daddy was quiet during breakfast but chatted with the camera crew from ESPN when they arrived in the late afternoon. His voice was strained; each careful word he spoke was a dam that held back the torrent of truth that might burst forth again at any moment.

The draft continued. Picks slipped away, one by one. Thirty-seven: safety from South Florida to the Philadelphia Eagles. Thirty-eight: Cleveland took a safety. Forty-nine: a safety. Toward the end of the second round, I caught Cory's eye. He shook his head in frustrated disbelief.

The third round replayed the same story. A safety at seventy-one, at seventy-five, at seventy-six. "I know I'm better than this guy," I thought. "I was ranked higher than him; I had more tackles than him. I started over him at the Senior Bowl. When we played against each other, one on one, I outplayed him for the whole week. But he gets drafted way ahead of me? What is going on?"

My name was not called that day. I went to bed early that night, wishing for the solace of sleep. Instead, a parade of images floated through my mind. I saw the dark sky of the mornings I'd woken before dawn to train with Cory; I saw the pile of football gear I'd arranged in my room at Teddy Hall; I saw my father's face as he watched Whitney run for a touchdown that day many years ago in Galloway; I saw a football floating toward me as I reached out to intercept it. I saw a lifetime of small improvements, thousands of incremental steps toward this goal. What good were they now?

● ● ●

On the last day of the draft, I traveled with my family back home to Galloway. We'd been sitting in Orlando for too many disappointing hours. I needed a change of scenery. The camera crews followed us back to the Rolle family home. We would bring it back to the beginning, to the living room where Cory and I had watched Deion Sanders as boys, the same room where Whitney had greased us up before we boxed, the yard where Rahlu and I had practiced my footwork.

The fourth round went by. Nothing. The clock ticked away. Guys from schools I had never heard of were getting drafted. Toward the end of the fifth round, Cory pulled me aside. "We're starting to think about free agency," he said.

If an NFL prospect goes undrafted, they can sign with a team as a free agent and try to fight for a roster spot. It's not a position any player wants to be in.

"How has it gotten to this point?" I asked. "I can't believe I'm thinking about being an undrafted free agent."

"You are going to be drafted. But we have to think about where we want to sign if it doesn't happen," Cory said, trying to focus on the practical matters at hand. "Where would you want to go?"

I glanced over at the camera crew. They seemed restless, looking at their phones and kicking the rug, bored. *I'm disappointing everybody*, I thought. *I'm even disappointing the cameramen.*

"I need to get out of this house," I told Cory.

"Where are you going to go?"

"I'm just going," I called over my shoulder as I stormed toward the door.

The film crews jumped into motion, happy for a bit of action. "Please don't follow me," I told them. "I need some time alone."

"You coming back?" asked a sound guy with a three-day beard. "We need to get the last shot."

I didn't answer him because I didn't know. I left the house and walked around the corner with no destination in mind. I remember exactly what I was wearing: gray slacks, black shoes, a white shirt with gray vertical stripes. A gust of wind mussed my open collar. The weather was sunny, maybe sixty-five degrees. At that moment, the dialogue in my head went like this: "*You aren't going to succeed. This will be the first failure of your life. You are going to fail, Myron.*"

I saw myself at twelve years old, writing down my goals. "*Get to the NFL and become a neurosurgeon. Neurosurgeon, NFL player, Neurosurgeon, NFL player.*" I had repeated the words so many times that they had become intractable from my identity. Who would I be if this dream didn't come true? What would be left of me if it vanished?

I realized I was walking fast. The wind whipped open a few buttons on my shirt. I must have looked crazed. I looked to see if anyone was around. The coast was clear: suburban houses and lawns sat quiet and contented all down the tree-lined block. For everyone else, it was just a regular Saturday. For me, it was the worst afternoon of my life.

At that awful moment, the last thing I wanted to do was try to make myself feel 2 percent better, 2 percent more in control of this situation and my emotions. I just wanted to run, run, run down the block and away from the disappointed faces that would greet me when I returned home. But I had to try. I tried to slow my breathing, telling myself, "God's got you. He's always had you before, and he will see you through this as well."

A modicum of calm entered my spirit. It was enough to grasp, enough to keep negative thoughts at bay long enough to replace them with a new script. "There's got to be a way, Myron," I said aloud to the afternoon air. I realized I was talking to myself on a street corner, but desperate times call for desperate measures. "You've done what you had to do. It's in his hands now. With him, it's going to be all right." I kept repeating that to myself to make it more real. I said it again, raising my voice. Nobody could hear me; it was just God and me. "There is a way. He has you. He has you." Speaking those words affirmed that I was still doing the right thing and holding on to his unchanging hand. It gave me enough strength to go back and face what I needed to face.

When I walked back into the house, I could see from everyone's furtive eyes that my name had not been called. Fatigue hit me. I bolted past the camera crew, past my family who looked at me with concern, toward my bedroom. "Please, don't come in here, don't bother me," I said before I shut the door.

I went to my childhood bed and lay down with my clothes on. Eventually, Rahlu came in. "Hey, Myron. They're playing your ESPN special," he said, keeping his voice low, the way I do now when I'm talking to a patient with a grave illness.

"Cool, that's good."

"Do you want to come and watch it with us?"

"No, I don't care to see it, man."

"All right, cool." He closed the door, and I fell into a fitful sleep.

After thirty minutes of tossing and turning, I got up again and sat on the couch to watch round six. Mummy was on my right side, Daddy was on my left, locking me into place. Needing something to do with my nervous hands, I texted my cousin Samari.

"Round six," I wrote. "I'm worried, man."

"Stay patient," Samari replied. "God is first. He's got you. You're a Rolle. They'll regret not drafting you sooner."

I was drafting my reply when my phone rang. A jolt of hope shot through me as I saw a strange number light up the screen.

"Better pick it up quick," Daddy said, his eyes alive.

"This is Myron Rolle."

"Hey, Myron, it's Jeff Fisher from the Tennessee Titans. How are you doing?"

"I'm doing well, coach."

As Coach Fisher spoke, I heard the sound I'd been waiting for: *da, da, ding.* "With the 207th pick in the 2010 NFL Draft, the Tennessee Titans select Myron Rolle."

"And there we have it, the Rhodes Scholar is selected," said ESPN's smiling talking head.

My family went crazy, jumping up and down and hugging. The camera crew got their shot. All the anxiety and disappointment of the last three days melted away in one moment of joy and vindication. Sure, it was the sixth round, but the NFL wanted me, the Tennessee Titans wanted me, Coach Fisher wanted me.

With the cameras rolling, I spoke to my new coach. "Oh, man," I said. "Hey, coach, how are you doing?"

"Are you ready to be a Titan?"

"Dang right I'm ready to be a Titan, coach."

"We'll see you at camp. Congratulations."

Cheers erupted before I hung up the phone. Mummy was crying. It should have happened earlier, but we got there together. I remembered what Senator Booker had told me about plans. *If you want God to laugh, tell him your plans.* I decided to focus on the positive and praise God for allowing my dream to come true. Myron Rolle: safety, Tennessee Titans. It had a nice ring to it.

After the camera crew went home, we had a big party. Mummy invited some of my teachers from elementary school and middle school. They hugged me, telling me how proud they were. It didn't matter to them if I was a first- or sixth-round pick. I was the boy who had sat in their classrooms and dreamed big.

A girl who grew up with us was a club promoter in Atlantic City, and she used her sway to host a draft party for me at Caesar's Palace. I called all my family back home in the Bahamas in the car on the way there. They already knew—the Bahamian broadcasting network ZNS was running the story as breaking news.

At Caesar's Palace, I sat down at a table chock-full of bottles stuffed with sparklers. I hugged some friends I grew up with in Jersey. The DJ gave me some love and called out my name, announcing that I had just gotten drafted into the National Football League. People in the club cheered and clapped. My friends convinced me to try my first glass of champagne. I drank only half of it: it was terrible.

Relief was my only emotion when my head hit the pillow that night. I'd gotten in the door. Samari had told me, "It doesn't matter whether you get in through the front door, the side door, or through a window—you're in the house."

A few days after the draft, ESPN's Jemele Hill called me to talk about a piece she was writing about why I had fallen so far in the draft. Hill, who would become one of the foremost writers about the intersections of race, sports, and culture for The Undefeated, had insights into the situation that few other journalists cared to examine.

"I'd love to see what the draft process is like in the back war rooms. What they're looking at, how they're evaluating players. There were a lot of guys taken ahead of me that I know I'm better than," I told her. "When my classmates at Oxford were drinking at the pubs or traveling to different parts of the EU, I was working out, training, going to sleep, resting my body, making sure I was ready to compete. I love this game. I love this sport, and I want it to be my vocation for the next ten years."[2]

Hill listened to my story with empathy. Once again, a strong Black woman had my back at a time when I needed it most. Her piece, published a few days later, articulated what had gone on behind the scenes. "I wish I could say Rolle's free fall was strictly football-related, but it's become apparent the biggest reason Rolle tumbled was that some NFL coaches and executives were unnerved by Rolle's tremendous off-field success, which included winning a Rhodes Scholarship," she wrote. "As unhealthy as it sounds, NFL coaches prefer players who won't challenge the league's well-established groupthink mentality. They value warriors, not thinkers. They want players who can't survive without football. They want players they can control and influence, and some of them might have felt intimidated if they thought they were coaching a player who was smarter than them."[3]

Being a Rhodes Scholar devalued me as a football player. That infuriates me to this day. When universities and coaches talk to the media, they constantly stress education. I had walked the path that America told me to walk, and still I was punished. What more did the world want from me? It hurt then, and it hurts recounting it now. There will always be a small crack there, where the pain seeped in.

It stings that the NFL questioned my commitment to the game I love so much. Florida State had supported my vision to be a scholar-athlete. But as soon as money became involved, priorities changed. Being an intelligent Black football player with options outside of football became a liability rather than an asset. It almost cost me my dream.

How you move forward from a setback is critical. Falling in the draft helped forge me. I now know more about sorrow. When I look back, I ask myself why the hurt attached to this moment was so profound. It's because I love football with every inch of myself. Today, my wife, Latoya, who didn't know me when I played ball, can still feel my innate connection to the game. "When you're watching football, it's like you're a different man," she tells me. But after the draft, I moved forward with a new resolve. I vowed that once I got to training camp, I would use the 2% Way to reward the Titans for believing in me and prove to all the doubters that I belonged in the NFL.

I have always been two men: a football player and a scholar. The world insisted that these two men were at odds with each other, but in my soul they moved as one. One could not have existed without the other. I wish the NFL could have seen that in 2010. Please know that you too do not have to box yourself into the mold the world demands. You may lose money. You may have people tell you that your goals don't make sense. Your friends and family may doubt you. But if you hold on to your inner light, that part of you that burns hot and true, it will eventually burst through. That's what light does. It shines.

Chapter 7

ONE OR THE OTHER

I stood in front of my locker at Saint Thomas Sports Park, the Tennessee Titans training facility in Nashville. Inside hung a baby blue jersey with *Rolle* emblazoned over the number 25. Above the locker, in a square cubby, a pristine white helmet waited, free, for the moment, of grass stains and pad marks. The Titans logo, a *T* with a trail of flames, flowed like a comet down its side.

I'd arrived in Nashville for rookie minicamp, a weekend-long intensive where I'd get my first taste of NFL life. The Titans facility spreads out over thirty-one acres: three outdoor practice fields and an indoor field fitted with artificial turf that simulated the environment of our AFC South bedfellows, the Indianapolis Colts. Masseuses waited at the ready to knead their knuckles into sore hamstrings. The film room was big enough to host a Hollywood movie premiere. Oversized model swords and back-lit signs that read "Storm the South" and "Grind It Out" decorated the hallways. The weight room seemed endless, and the clang of metal plates emanated from it day and night.

I reached into my locker and grabbed my jersey, pulling it over my shoulder pads. I'd spent most of my life in some manner of football uniform. This was different. I felt like a superhero donning his suit. I picked up my helmet, ready for combat, ready to take my place among the chosen few who play on Sunday.

I played well in rookie camp, snatching two interceptions. The speed and physicality on the field were considerably higher than in the college game. Quickness and ferocity were the cornerstones of my game: the pro game played to my strengths. Still, I was one of eight rookies fighting to earn their spot, six of whom had been picked ahead of me in the draft. I faced an uphill battle to see my name on the final fifty-three-man roster.

Fifty-three is a number every NFL player knows by heart. It's an ironclad rule in the league: only fifty-three players make the active roster. Eight players can remain on the practice squad and do not travel with the team to away games. If you're not one of the fifty-three, you're fighting for your life every snap.

After rookie camp, those snaps can be hard to come by. Casual fans might not be aware of the complicated dynamics that determine playing time for rookies. It's not a straightforward meritocracy. How many opportunities a player gets to perform and how quickly they are put into the starting lineup or the rotation can have very little to do with pure skill. It has more to do with investment. High draft picks needed to be given chances because the Titans had wagered significant capital on them. General manager Mike Reinfeldt and owner Bud Adams wanted to see their dollars and decisions on the field. An undrafted rookie who comes in and dominates has less of a chance of making the squad than a high draft pick who has underperformed. Nobody wants egg on their face or to admit they backed up the money truck for a bust. That gets general managers fired.

I couldn't change this system, but I could do my best to survive it. I wrote the number 53 in my journal, circled it, then circled it again.

• • •

After rookie camp, I headed back to Orlando, rejoining trainer Tom Shaw's legendary speed camp. Shaw had revolutionized conditioning in the early 2000s and served on Bill Belichick's staff, winning three Super Bowls with the Patriots. My group consisted of a handful of college standouts getting ready for the combine and twenty-five NFL players, including a cadre of Steelers players and fellow Titan Chris Johnson. In 2009 Johnson won the NFL rushing title with 2,006 yards and broke Marshall Faulk's single-season record of total yards from scrimmage, earning him the nickname CJ2K.

We had an excellent cohort of alpha-male ballers pushing one another every day. We started with straight-ahead speed drills, improving our times by fractions of a second. Soon I was running faster than I had at rookie camp. Shaw ran me through safety-specific drills: I practiced reading the quarterback, getting to the hash mark—my landmark—backpedaling, turning, finding the ball, finding the receiver, seeing the high point of the ball, catching it in the air, and spitting it back for a pick-six. I absorbed the work ethic, the techniques, and the grind from NFL players around the league. The Steelers guys loved the 2% Way, and as the weeks went on, we measured our improvements. Everyone got faster, smarter, and more ready for a league that takes no prisoners and accepts no excuses.

• • •

The sweat I spent in Shaw's camp paid off. I ran blistering speeds on my initial conditioning tests with the Titans, making a good first impression at training camp.

The level of intensity notched up tenfold when the veteran Titans reported to camp. Quarterback Vince Young had been named the NFL's Comeback Player of the Year the previous season and was slated to appear on the cover of the latest *Madden NFL* video game.

A *Madden* cover is a cultural honor every player covets despite the legendary "Madden Curse," which claims, with some good examples, that whoever appears on the game's cover will soon fall from grace. In 2010 Young was one of the few starting Black quarterbacks in the NFL, continuing a legacy that Warren Moon had begun back in 1984 when he became the first Black QB to lead the franchise, then named the Oilers. Young was explosive and capable of big plays, and we believed in him as our leader. I was glad to see a Black man in that role.

Pro-Bowlers Jason Babin, a defensive end, and Michael Griffin, a free safety, were the big dogs on defense. I marveled at the way they read plays, always at the right place at the right time. I knew I was capable of that acumen, and from a physical standpoint, I felt right in the mix.

The lifestyle change was the biggest adjustment. Nothing can fully prepare you for life in the NFL. Everything is oversized: the stadiums, the egos, the paychecks of some of the players. Instead of the sense of brotherhood I had while playing the college game, I saw individuality bordering on selfishness. It's a multibillion-dollar business, and players get a good piece of that pie. Players are brands. And brands don't always get along with other brands. They compete with them.

I've never held that mindset. The average NFL career lasts a little over three years. One year a player can be making a million dollars; the next, they could blow out their knee and never be called back to the league.

If a player hasn't set himself up for the long term, what options does he have? He just went from having a seven-figure salary to making five figures as an assistant coach somewhere. Guys have to provide for their families and will do what they have to do to keep themselves relevant, whether it's playing through an injury or just looking out for themselves.

I accepted the business-minded reality of the pro game but still wanted to connect with my teammates. I'd try with the older guys on the team, the vets who could impart some wisdom. Because I have four older brothers who have always steered me right, I gravitate toward mature people. Those are usually the ones from whom you can learn 2 percent.

Before I had much of a chance to speak to *anyone*, the Titans put me through media training. Team publicity officials instructed us to give stock answers to reporters' questions. "This helps avoid headlines that might distract the team," they explained. As I sat through the briefings, making my mouth form the words others had written for it, something didn't sit right with me. "I can think on my own," I thought. "I can see things for what they are and opine on them as a human with a brain." Since fifth grade, I'd always been vocal about my desire to be a neurosurgeon *and* an NFL player. I'd always been truthful about any subject I'd been asked about by reporters. My considered, nuanced answers had earned me the nickname "president" from my teammates at FSU. I took pride in that nickname. Now I was expected to divert, deflect, obfuscate. "Bite your tongue if you need to," I told myself. "Make the roster."

When training camp started, the depth chart listed me as the fourth-string safety. I wouldn't have much of a chance to prove myself if I never saw the field. I broke out my goals into accomplishable chunks and made a second column that listed actions I could take to improve by 2 percent.

1. **GOAL**: *Improve my strength to NFL starter level*
   2% WAY: *Extra workout before practice; eat clean; use all resources available to maintain health*
2. **GOAL**: *Build teammate relationships*
   2% WAY: *Find vets to learn from; stay away from guys who party; find Christians on the team*
3. **GOAL**: *Show coaches you're committed to football*
   2% WAY: *Watch tape at home; be a team player; don't mention any subjects other than football in interviews or meetings*

That last item gave me pause, but I was monomaniacally focused on being one of the fifty-three. I devised a schedule that would allow me the time to make these 2 percent improvements. I rose each morning at five o'clock and arrived at the Titans facility by six, where I squeezed in an early workout. The other guys doing squats before breakfast nodded at me as they added plates to their racks. By seven o'clock, I had eaten a protein-packed breakfast and was ready for a series of offensive meetings, defensive back meetings, and special teams meetings. Then I practiced for two hours, hustling through every whistle. In the afternoon, we had more team meetings, and then most of the guys hit the hot tub. I lifted again, ate, and stretched.

That level of activity, day after day, is hard on the body. I made sure to spend the late afternoon rehabilitating in contrasting hot and cold tubs. Hot, cold, hot, cold until your muscles relax and begin to heal. Then I went to our masseuse, watching tape as he worked on me, and did yoga in the afternoon as well. After a final film session, I ate dinner and arrived back to my apartment at seven o'clock, fourteen hours after leaving home. I looked over my playbook again, watched some film, and then got enough sleep to have the energy to restart the day. Repeat. Repeat. Repeat.

Once again, the 2% Way paid dividends. By the time preseason started, I was the number two safety on the depth chart, behind only our starter. That meant playing time. In our first preseason game against the Seattle Seahawks, I had a few pass breakups and a couple of big hits that concluded excellent defensive plays. We won our next preseason game against the St. Louis Rams. Instead of going to the club, I headed to the gym to celebrate with dead lifts.

Spending every waking moment at Saint Thomas Sports Park allowed me to check off another goal on my list: connecting with my teammates. Safeties Vinnie Fuller and Chris Hope and linebacker David Thornton were seasoned vets with at least six years in the league. They took me under their wings like a little brother.

Instead of trying to get a hotel party cracking after practice, these guys showed me the local church. Football players go to church on Wednesday; we're otherwise occupied on Sunday. There I joined a Bible study and grew close to Bishop Joseph Walker, who brought us to his house and fed us like family. As we broke bread, my team-mates, Bishop Walker, and I talked about Christianity and marriage. Temptation is laid at your feet when you're a pro ballplayer. We could succumb to it, or we could learn how to walk carefully and avoid the minefield.

We split the next two games against the Panthers and Saints, ending the preseason at 2–2. When I checked the stat sheet, I led the squad in tackles. "That ought to get me on the team," I thought, pleased with my development. Linebacker coach Dave McGinnis validated those feelings. He came up to me while I was shivering away in an ice bath and said, "You know, I've been coaching foot-ball for longer than you've been alive, and you can play eight years in this league." My defensive back coach, Marcus Robertson, echoed those thoughts when he told me, "You know, I can see an eight-year career for you. I really do."

Making the fifty-three-man roster no longer seemed to be in question. In my mind, I shifted my goal. I wanted to get one NFL start, even if it was on special teams.

● ● ●

It was Saturday. I was doing shoulder presses with the rest of the rookies. I lowered the barbell, pushed out my set, and racked it. I felt a tap on my shoulder. I went cold. Nobody in the NFL ever wants to feel a tap on the shoulder. *Maybe it's just another player wanting to use the rack.*

Our assistant strength coach stood above me. "Hey, Myron," he said. "Can you come with me for a second? Bring your playbook."

Oof.

My teammate, who had been spotting me, mumbled, "Dang, bro," under his breath. He knew the deal.

"This can't be happening," I thought as I took the long walk to Coach Fisher's office. "I've been playing so well. Two days ago, I blitzed off the end and knocked a running back off his feet."

From behind his desk, Coach Fisher grimaced under his cowboy mustache. He got right to the point. "Myron, you're playing well," he said. "No one expected you to be doing as well as you're doing after having a year and a half off. But I think it needs a little bit more time. We're going to put you on a practice squad."

A year and a half off. The phrase followed me like a hex. I thanked Coach and returned to the weight room, steaming. My teammates gave me a wide berth as I obliterated the rest of the shoulder set. I'd barely escaped the ax. Now I waited in limbo with seven other guys on the practice squad. We could be cut or picked up by another team at any moment and wouldn't travel with the team to away games. *No one expected you to be doing this well.* The words echoed in my head as I slammed another plate onto each end of the barbell. *Why not?*

● ● ●

Making the practice squad was better than a ticket back to Galloway. My position on the team didn't reflect my play, but I had to make the best of my situation. I still had NFL snaps under my belt. I was still pulling an NFL paycheck. I was still a Titan. "Let's go after it," I resolved. "Let's get better."

Being on the practice squad meant I would be on the scout team defense during the week when the offense practiced. I intercepted passes left and right, making plays all over the field. After I blew up one of his carefully orchestrated schemes, Jeff Fisher called me over and said, "Myron, you're out here interrupting and disrupting all our plays, huh?"

After that, they used me differently on the scout team. Every week in scrimmages, when we were going up against a team with a star on defense, I played that role. If we were playing the Steelers, I would be Troy Polamalu for the week. I blitzed like Troy. I moved around, and I acted crazy like him. When we played the Baltimore Ravens, I was Ed Reed for the week. I was back at safety, doing all his tricky zones and reads. Even if we were due to face an outstanding linebacker, I became a linebacker for that week to imitate their best player.

The coaches realized I could play at this level, but something held them back from elevating me. I couldn't understand what it was. When an injury happened, other defensive guys would get pushed up ahead of me. When our safety went down in week eight, I was not called up.

I was baffled, but I tried not to let it phase me. I put forth maximum effort to get 2 percent better every day at practice so that when my time came, I could go out there and show everyone what I was capable of.

In my bones, I knew I belonged on that field. My teammates saw it. They believed it. But something held me back: an invisible force that prevented the Titans coaching staff from letting me ball, letting me cook, letting me do my thing. I wasn't placed on the active roster in any of the sixteen games that year.

We went 6–10 for the season, 2–4 in the AFC South, landing at the bottom of the division. Coach Fisher resigned shortly after the season ended. Vince Young, who in week eleven had thrown his shoulder pads into the crowd and had a shouting match with Fisher afterward in the locker room, never suited up in Titan blue again. It was a rough season. Rougher times lay just around the corner as I clung to one of the eight spots in no-man's-land, hanging by a thread.

• • •

In March 2011, a few months before training camp was set to convene, tensions boiled over between the owners and the players. For the next eighteen weeks, the owners imposed a lockout while the player's association negotiated a new collective bargaining agreement. I was still on the Titans practice roster but was barred from reporting to work, as was the rest of the league.

I used the time to take President Clinton up on the offer he had extended when I won the Rhodes to participate in a Clinton Global Initiative to combat sexual violence in Congo and Rwanda. Our group, which included Ashley Judd and Jeff Gordon, traveled to Africa to petition the government, lobby, and get involved in policy and advocacy. I spoke to Dr. Denis Mukwege at Panzi Hospital, who had won a Nobel Prize for treating African women who had been raped. I visited a women's shelter where they taught women literacy skills, including financial literacy. They empowered Congolese women by teaching them about the laws that protect them. "We were abused when we were young girls, but we're stronger than that," the women told us. "That moment won't define us."

Africa changed me for the better. After hearing those women's stories, I resolved to make global health a priority when I began my medical career. On the plane ride back to Nashville, I wondered how the football world would perceive my trip. "*Taking more time away from the game,*" I imagined scouts scribbling on their reports. Toward the end of my first season, *Sporting News* had named me the second most intelligent player in sports, a distinction I was honored to receive. Would everyone see it that way? Would owners take it as yet another sign that I didn't need football? Would they worry that my intelligence might spill out into interviews, that I might actually answer questions on social issues?

In July the players and the owners reached a new collective bargaining agreement. The Titans returned to work with some new faces in the mix. Mike Munchak, who had previously been the offensive line coach with the Steelers, replaced Jeff Fisher as head coach. Because I was a player on the periphery, a new coach made me wary. Jeff Fisher had drafted me, not Mike Munchak.

The first week of camp, Coach Munchak went down the stretch lines talking to all the players. As I stretched my quads, I could hear him walking up and down, speaking to every player about their tackling ability, their blocking, their hand placement and asking about their weight.

When he got to me, he smiled and said, "Hey, Myron. How was President Clinton?"

He had spent the last fifteen minutes talking football with the rest of the Titans. But I got the President Clinton humanitarian talk.

"You know President Clinton, he's an Arkansas Razorback," I said, trying to turn the conversation back to the gridiron. "The Razorback football squad is playing well this year, and it means a lot to him. And football means a lot to me. That's why I'm out here trying to compete."

"You'll have to tell me all about him someday," Coach Munchak said before moving on to talk to one of our tight ends.

My work in Africa affected the questions I fielded from the media. Beat writers for teams typically ask about trades, acquisitions, rookies, changes in stat charts, and injury reports. That I'd never hidden my desire to be a neurosurgeon put a label on me that was hard to shake: I had more to me than only the sport. Reporters wouldn't ask, "Hey, Myron, how did you find that receiver in a Cover Two?" They'd ask, "Myron, so how do you know Cornel West?" At the time, I wished they would've asked about our plans to defend Peyton Manning the following week. That would have helped my mission of busting down the stigmatization that I couldn't be a serious person and a ballplayer.

Throughout the preseason, the line of questioning remained the same. When beat reporters asked about health care in the United States or traumatic brain injury, I tried to turn the answers back to sports. Most of the public now understands, having witnessed what happened to Colin Kaepernick, that politics can derail an athlete's career no matter how good he is. The owners do not want outspoken players in the NFL.

Remember, I played for the Titans back in 2011. Kap hadn't yet opened those gates. I worried that if I spoke up, I would be a distraction from the military-like atmosphere of a football franchise.

We finished the preseason 3–1, and our team felt like we had the right pieces in place to improve our record. I hoped I would be one of those pieces come cut day. Cut day is the deadline when teams have to whittle their roster down to that magic number of fifty-three. In the hours before cut day, talk about "the grim reaper" floated around the Titans facilities. Not all of us would be there come the next morning.

For me, the grim reaper took the form of Titans vice president of football operations, Lake Dawson. Dawson called me into his office and said, "Myron, you've got a lot of really good tape this year on film. Maybe even better than last year."

"So what is the problem?" I thought.

"I've seen you grow," he said. "I've seen your progress. But, you know, it's a numbers thing. We're going to keep more corners than safeties this year."

"Thank you for the opportunity."

The grim reaper took my playbook, and that was that. I was no longer a Tennessee Titan.

● ● ●

After another shorter, curter meeting with Coach Munchak, I cleaned out my locker for the last time at Saint Thomas Sports Park. Luckily, I had a duffel bag with me. The NFL is notorious for cutting guys on such short notice that they leave with their things in a plastic garbage bag. One moment you're on a team plane headed for a stadium full of fans, the next you're waiting at the bus stop holding a Hefty bag. I took one final look around the locker room, noticing that at least a dozen were newly vacant. The grim reaper had had a busy morning.

As I took the long walk toward the exit, Steve Watterson, our head strength coach, appeared in my path. "Myron, I just heard. I can't believe it."

"I can't make sense of it either."

"Some of these cuts I saw coming. But you?"

"Thanks, Coach."

"I want you out there, man."

"Somebody else doesn't," I said, pointing a finger skyward.

We both knew what I had implied: ownership. I hadn't yet connected all the dots, but I felt that the old stigmas that had begun when I accepted the Rhodes were still working against me, keeping me from what I wanted most in the world.

I boarded the next coach flight back to Orlando. The guy in front of me, who wore a Titans hat, put his seat back after takeoff, jamming my knees.

● ● ●

There's an old saying in the league: "You haven't played long enough if you haven't gotten cut." Though demoralizing, it's a routine part of football life. Richard Sherman, Peyton Manning, Dez Bryant, and Tim Tebow have all handed over their playbooks. Those are the names we remember. Thousands of guys slip from the depth chart into obscurity, memorialized only by a few stats on a webpage nobody visits.

The Titans had cut my cousin Samari Rolle in 2005 for salary cap reasons. He'd gone on to play four more productive seasons with the Baltimore Ravens. Samari assured me that I'd get another shot in the league.

I knew I still had football in front of me. A few weeks later, I got a call from an unknown number with a 412 area code.

"Hey, Myron. Mike Tomlin from the Pittsburgh Steelers."

There was no other person on earth, besides maybe Bill Belichick, that I wanted to be on the other end of that line. Under Tomlin's stewardship as head coach, the Steelers had gone 12–4 in 2008. Their formula for success was a physical defense that allowed the fewest points, passing yards, and total yards in the league. First Team All-Pro strong safety and 2010 Defensive Player of the Year Troy Polamalu captained that defense. If I made the cut in Pittsburgh, I would have a chance to learn under the very best.

"Hey, Coach," I said, trying to keep my voice even. "How are you doing?"

"Doing well, Myron. I remember watching you at Florida State. I'd like for you to have a look at us here in Pittsburgh. We'll bring you up here for a tryout. See what you can do."

"I appreciate that, Coach. That means a lot."

So I went up to Pittsburgh to see what I could do. It turns out I could do a lot. They signed me on the spot.

• • •

The Steelers held training camp at Saint Vincent College in Latrobe, Pennsylvania. The town of eight thousand lies in the western foothills of Pennsylvania's Allegheny Mountains. No distractions. Just ball. Once again I focused on small improvements and worked my way to being a starter on the preseason squad.

Our first preseason game would be a Pennsylvania battle: Steelers versus Eagles. Classic hard-nosed football. Since the game was in Philly, my parents came to watch me play. I couldn't wait to get out there in my black-and-yellow uniform and hit somebody with Daddy watching.

And hit people I did. I specifically remember one punt return.

I was running down on punt coverage at full steam. The punt returner caught the ball, took two steps, and I launched at him like a missile. Daddy said he could hear the crack of the hit from his seat.

After the game, we Steelers loaded onto the team bus and headed for the airport. I sat behind our starting linebacker Larry Foote. Larry Foote wasn't someone anyone trifled with if they valued their health. Picture Deebo from *Friday*, but from the streets of Detroit. I hadn't spoken one word to Foote all through camp, minicamp, or preseason. That was fine with me. When Foote spoke, he was usually putting his foot in you.

Foote took his headphones out of his ears and turned around to face me when I sat down. He looked at me and said, "Hey, Rolle."

"Larry?" I asked, cautiously.

"You balled out there tonight."

"Appreciate that."

He turned around and put his headphones back in.

A warm feeling of validation spread through my tired body. To hear those words from a guy like Larry Foote, whose usual language was silence or doling out physical pain on the field, meant more than a hundred glowing ESPN articles.

We won the rest of our preseason games, finishing 3–1. In our last preseason game against the Carolina Panthers, I felt off my game. I failed to record a tackle for the first time in my NFL career. One game shouldn't have sunk me, but cut day loomed around the corner. I could hear the grim reaper sharpening his scythe. The next day, as I watched *SportsCenter* in the team hotel, my phone rang. "Come see us," a voice intoned.

"Sure thing," I said and began to put down the receiver.

"Wait . . . Rolle."

"Yes?" I asked, snapping the phone back to my ear, a piece of hope sneaking its way into my chest.

"Bring your playbook."

On Monday morning, I said goodbye to Coach Tomlin. "Sorry things shook out this way. I would have kept you, but it wasn't up to me," he said. "I'm not worried about you, Myron. You can be president if you want to."

I wanted to say, "All I want to do right now is play football." The NFL had made its message clear: *Go be a doctor. Go be the president. We don't care—but not the NFL. You can't do both.* After three years I hadn't been able to convince the league that it didn't have to be one or the other. There was no use trying now.

I cleared out my locker, taking my shoulder pads with me as a memento. I chucked them in the back of my black GMC Terrain and got behind the wheel. "Where do I go now?" I wondered. Nearly every moment of my life up until that point had been regimented, accounted for. Freedom felt foreign, terrifying.

There was only one answer: home. I got on I-76 and headed east. Hundreds of miles slipped by in sorrow. Three years, and I'd never appeared in a single NFL game. I thought about all the people back in the Bahamas that would be disappointed that one of their own hadn't made it in the NFL. The fields of the Pennsylvania Dutch Country gave way to the metal and concrete of Philadelphia. I crossed the New Jersey border, the scenery growing more and more familiar. At last I pulled into my parents' driveway.

Mummy was waiting with a plate of peas 'n' rice.

• • •

In the book of Exodus, the Israelites wandered the desert for forty years. The children of God were lost in a wasteland of despair and sand that seemed to go on without end.

For thirty days after the Steelers cut me, I too wandered, directionless. Football, the sport I'd loved passionately since my memory began, had been taken away from me. For years I had risen before dawn; now I pulled the shades down when the sun tried to rouse me from my childhood bed. I lost my appetite. In my lowest moments, I regretted taking the Rhodes Scholarship.

Worried, my brothers dropped by to check on me. They'd never seen me this lost. Cory brought an offer from the Canadian Football League. I rejected it outright.

Sometimes I'd catch a glimpse of myself in the mirror. I was unfamiliar with the downcast look that played across my face, but I still saw 212 pounds of chiseled muscle. I knew I could still play football. I felt it. "Am I really done?" I asked myself. "Do I really want to walk away forever?"

Small rays of solace appeared in the form of calls from my former teammates. Ryan Clark, an undrafted free agent who went on to win a Super Bowl, was the first to reach out. "I'm shocked that this happened," he said.

"I'm not," I replied.

"Bro, this was not you, this was not you. It has nothing to do with your playing."

"You did nothing out there to embarrass yourself. You played very well."

Troy Polamalu, who was inducted as a first-ballot Hall of Famer in 2020, had a similar reaction. "You were out here balling. What is going on?" he asked.

"I'm not sure, brother," I replied.

"Bro, try not to take it personally. If you want to keep playing, keep balling, man."

"I'll think about it."

"You've done well," he said. "I mean that."

"Thank you."

"Let me know where you land."

My cousin Samari Rolle also reached out. "I was in the league a long time," he said. "I've seen a lot of guys come and go. You are d—well good enough to be on an NFL roster. You're smart enough to lead a defense. Or at the very least a special teams unit."

"Maybe I was too smart," I said.

"When was the last time you heard a GM say a white quarterback was too smart?" Samari asked.

I laughed bitterly.

"I'm just laying out the facts," Samari said. "You see how the media talks about Peyton Manning? The way he prepares. That he's like a technician. You never see them saying he's too smart, do you?"

"I feel you," I said.

"There's nothing you did to deserve this," he said. "Pro football is a hard game. It comes and goes. But look at the future you have in front of you. Most guys don't know what they want to do when they get out of the league."

"I hope . . . I hope I didn't let you down."

"Get those words out of your mouth," Samari said. "I'm a football player, same as you. We both know what this is. You don't realize how proud you've made all of us."

"Thank you," I said, my throat growing thick.

"Hey, Myron."

"Yeah, Samari?"

"Stay smart."

In the NFL, true acceptance comes from your teammates and other players who have walked the walk. To hear my brothers, guys who had succeeded at the highest level, saying what I had never heard from management lifted doubt from my troubled soul. It confirmed that my play hadn't been what kept me off the field on Sunday.

Those conversations clarified my experience in the NFL and what I might expect from another go-around. If my performance wasn't to blame, then the nebulous assumptions that began swirling around me from the moment I took the Rhodes had calcified into an impenetrable wall. There was no reason to think it would change. I would never get a fair shot.

"Why do I want to keep running this race?" I asked myself. "Shaking the stigma that I don't care about football is taking more energy than I'm expending on the field."

In Exodus, God did not arbitrarily curse the Israelites to wander the desert. God punished them for not obeying his orders to take the promised land of Canaan as their own. God had promised them victory. God will never lead us where his grace cannot provide for us or his power cannot protect us. They simply had to trust and obey, but this they did not do.

I wondered if I had been making the same mistake. "God, if you're telling me that it's time to move on, I'll listen," I prayed, dropping to my knees.

A knock sounded on my door, followed by Mummy's soft footsteps. She approached the spot where I knelt on the floor, holding a tattered notebook.

"Myron," she said, "I found this while going through some of your old things. It's your notebook from when you were young."

I stood, taking the journal into my hands. The binding had gone soft with the long years. I opened it to the first page. I saw a list written in my boyhood hand. I had added only two items.

When you grow up . . .

1. Play football in the NFL
2. Become a neurosurgeon

"I must have been in fifth grade when I wrote this," I said, showing Mummy the page.

She traced my pencil marks with a finger. "This one is done," she said, tapping the first entry. "You made good on it. Can we cross it off?"

I couldn't speak. I reached toward the bedside table and found a pen. Slowly, my hands shaking, I drew a red line across my first dream. When the tip of the pen reached the *L* in NFL, I felt a weight sucked from my body.

"Now this one," Mummy said, taking the pen from me and circling the word *neurosurgeon*. "We still have some work to do. But I think you're just the man for the job."

I stood, feeling the finality of the first part of my life flow into the promise of the next. Purpose began to replace despair. There was much to be done. I went out that day and got an MCAT practice book.

● ● ●

Years later I was in the Bahamas with my cousin Dr. Delon Brennen. As we sat and looked out at the water, our conversation drifted toward my days of playing pro ball.

"Do you know why you didn't get a fair shot in the NFL?" he asked me.

"I've got a few ideas," I replied.

"I know," he said. "They were nervous Dr. Rolle would talk about head injuries."

With the benefit of hindsight, this explanation makes sense. In 2009, just before I entered the league, *GQ* correspondent Jeanne Marie Laskas published the bombshell story "Game Brain," which profiled a team of scientists who proved that concussions in pro football players can lead to dementia. The NFL denied the findings, threatening to sue anyone who defamed the league. A slew of negative press followed.

Then in 2012, while I was with the Steelers, an unthinkable tragedy struck. Junior Seau, a Super Bowl champion who had been one of the faces of the league, took his own life by shooting himself in the chest. It was later confirmed that he suffered from an accumulation of abnormal brain protein secondary to repetitive concussive episodes. This condition is called chronic traumatic encephalopathy

(CTE). Suddenly, talk about traumatic brain injury and concussions was thrust to the forefront of the national conversation. The league looked negligent.

Enter Myron Rolle, a bright young kid who'd studied medical anthropology. Owners and general managers knew I was going into neurosurgery. I'd been vocal about it. Guys in the league already called me Dr. Rolle. One time a teammate called me up late at night, wanting medical advice. "Man, my younger brother, he got hit in the head in a car accident, and he's got a brain bleed. Can you tell me what I can do?"

"I'm not a doctor yet," I told him, trying to calm him down once I ascertained that the youngster was already in the hospital.

Thankfully, that kid survived. Not all NFL players are as lucky. Seau, sadly, was the tip of the iceberg. New studies had found CTE in the brains of other deceased former NFL players. Conditions like dementia, rage, and depression were being linked to head trauma incurred on the field, and the NFL was getting knocked for not protecting former players.

If I had gotten a head injury in the National Football League and that prevented me from becoming a neurosurgeon, it would have been national news. The NFL would take a massive hit on their popularity, on their image, on their ability to protect players, even current players.

So, from what I gathered, the powers that be were nervous about me. I think they figured it was only a matter of time before I spoke up about head trauma. The irony is that I went out of my way *not* to speak on social issues during my time in the league.

That's my one regret from my time in the NFL. Seeing what athletes in the NFL and NBA have done to raise their voices today, I wish I would have used my platform to elevate mine. I missed opportunities to speak on what mattered to me.

If I were to do it again, I would use my platform like Colin Kaepernick had done when he took a knee. But during my playing days, I wasn't yet ready to be the leader that Kaepernick was. I was so focused on applying the 2% Way to football that I hadn't immersed myself in social issues to a level where I felt comfortable advocating for them in front of television cameras. Kaepernick knew how the history of "The Star-Spangled Banner" connected to chattel slavery. He knew it took less time to graduate from the police academy than it took to become a hairdresser. Even his choice of clothes furthered his message.

I could have spent my time educating myself on CTE, becoming 2 percent more knowledgeable about how head injuries correlate with rates of suicide. I could have learned 2 percent more about how women in the Congo form community in the face of sexual violence. I could have inspired 2 percent of casual football fans to take action.

The next time I have a platform, I won't shy away. I'll make my voice heard. I owe that to football, and to myself.

Chapter 8

A ROOKIE AGAIN

I was twenty-six years old when I stepped away from the NFL. For the first time in my life, the world didn't expect me to be an athlete. When I woke in the morning, my first thought was, "Time for practice." There was no more practice. There never would be again.

It took time for my body to understand this new reality. My legs wanted to run sprints when I passed a field or a park. My muscles didn't know why I wasn't forcing them to heave huge amounts of weight. They were used to ripping and growing. If I was crossing the street and a car made a sudden lurch, or if Cory threw me my keys as I left the house, muscle memory took over, my heart rate spiked, and I waited for a hit.

I missed doling out those hits, but I was glad I no longer had to take them. As I studied for the MCAT, I took stock of my situation. What had football cost me? What had it left me that I could use going forward? I'd been fortunate: no concussions. I had all my faculties intact, and a stack of MCAT practice booklets resharpened the mental pathways I'd forged at Oxford. My hands—every surgeon's livelihood—had escaped uninjured, still full of dexterity. I had enough left of my NFL salary to lessen the financial burden of medical school.

Many athletes are lost when they leave the NFL. I threw myself headlong into medical school. It was a pleasure to snap back into study mode. I'd always had to balance academics with athletics. Now I had time to focus on one. My MCAT scores reflected that, and I was accepted into my first choice: Florida State University College of Medicine. They gave me the best scholarship, and I was going back to a familiar campus—I knew all the deans and professors. A Seminole again.

I entered medical school at age twenty-seven. I wasn't interested in decorating my dorm or throwing the frisbee on the quad. I'd already had more than my share of adventures at Florida State, the local papers documenting most of them. I wasn't going back to school so much as I was pursuing a means to an end: neurosurgery.

Being back at Florida State was a bit strange. People wanted to talk more about my being in the NFL than the cadaver we were dissecting in anatomy. But soon I felt a sense of community that I had missed while in the league.

Much of my first year consisted of nonclinical classroom work— books and dummies with plastic organs and learning the foundations of internal medicine. I wanted to get a jump start on the skills I'd need in the operating room. I began with the basics and focused on adding 2 percent each day.

Neurosurgeons need to be functionally ambidextrous. I'm right-handed, so I started writing with my left hand. My lefty handwriting looked like a child's but gradually improved. I went to the store and bought rubber strips. I'd make an incision with a pair of scissors, then suture it back together with shoelaces. When I watched my Seminoles play on Saturdays, I wound twine around my leg, practicing tying surgical knots.

My MacGyver-esque training improved my skills, and I steadily racked up credits in the classroom. But it would take more than rubber and shoelaces to make it in, arguably, the most demanding field in all of medicine. Neurosurgery is so competitive that some form of this question is in many application materials: *Consider whether you would be happy in any other field of medicine. If the answer is yes, perhaps neurosurgery is not the specialty for you.*

I'd known the answer to that question since the fifth grade.

Florida State medical school is known for producing primary care doctors who help serve rural areas in the state. A key mission of the school is being patient-centered, focused on serving *all* communities. This attracted me, as I had plans to treat underserved populations. But it also meant there was barely any coverage on the basics of neurosurgery. I knew I had to take the initiative to increase my knowledge and exposure to the field.

I asked around and met a neurosurgeon who let me observe his operations. Then through another contact I was introduced to Dr. Jay Storm, the head of pediatric neurosurgery at Children's Hospital of Philadelphia. Dr. Storm had trained under Dr. Ben Carson. Dr. Storm let me observe him perform a resection of a clival chordoma and do bench work in his lab. When I returned from Philly, I looked up neurosurgeons in South Florida who had good reputations and medical conferences in Orlando. On my weekends, I went and shook hands, gleaning as much knowledge as I could.

Most doctors told me the same thing: find away rotations, also known as externships, where I could spend thirty days in hospitals away from FSU's campus, working on long, complicated cases. Neurosurgery residencies are few, and matching someone who is not only intelligent and skilled but fits in well and will excel with the team is the goal of nearly every program, they said. If I could demonstrate this over a month-long visiting rotation, word would spread about me through program directors.

Typically, medical students do two away rotations. Beginning in my third year, I set out to do four.

As a fan of southern Florida, I was happy to find a neurosurgery program at Martin Memorial Medical Center on Florida's southeastern coast where I could shadow top neurosurgeons like Dr. John

Robinson and Dr. John Afshar. I often picked up extra hours working graveyard shifts at St. Lucie Medical Center, a hospital nearby. One hot night, I staffed an all-night surgical rotation shadowing Dr. Rene Loyola, a vascular surgeon.

Dr. Loyola was an affable Cuban man, good-natured even when we'd been at the hospital so long that time had lost meaning and everyone had bad coffee breath. That night I followed Dr. Loyola to the bed of a middle-aged woman with thinning sandy-blonde hair. Deep lines were etched in her face like a road map of a care-worn life. Dr. Loyola explained that years of smoking had caused severe plaque buildup in her arteries, leading to a series of small heart attacks and strokes.

"Her carotid artery is partially blocked," Dr. Loyola said. "We need to clear it out. It's a surgery I've done hundreds of times, but she has a lot of comorbidities. We need to take extra precautions."

We scrubbed in, and I assisted Dr. Loyola as he cleared out blood flow pathways through her compromised vascular system. The surgery was successful, but as I drove back to the student housing in Jupiter, a coastal town about thirty minutes away from the hospital, I couldn't shake the image of the woman's plaque-ridden arteries. She had survived, but her body was far from healthy, and I worried about her lying alone in the ICU, the beeps of the electronic vital sign monitor the only sound registering her existence.

My concern was well-founded. A few nights later, just after eleven o'clock, Dr. Loyola and I received a call that the woman was going downhill fast. We hurried to her bedside, where she lay alone and emaciated. She had been intubated—the tube running into her trachea was keeping her alive. It wouldn't keep her alive for much longer. She had reached the point where her body could no longer withstand any further medical intervention.

"Did you contact the family?" Dr. Loyola asked the ICU nurse. The nurse shook her head. Either she hadn't been able to contact a relative, or nobody had wanted to come. "They didn't even want to say goodbye?" I thought as Dr. Loyola sat down next to the woman and took her hand. It was just us—two men she barely knew would be the only witnesses to her last moments.

Dr. Loyola spoke softly into her ear, patting her on the head. I watched her heartbeat falling on the vital sign monitor. The beeps emanating from the machine lengthened. *Boop. Boooop. Boooooop.*

"Can I speak to her?" I asked, knowing there wasn't much time left.

Dr. Loyola made room for me. I took the woman's hand and told her, "It's going to be okay. You lived a good life. You fought a good fight. We're here. There's somebody here." I wanted her to know she wasn't alone.

We spoke to her until she flatlined. Dr. Loyola declared the time of death: 11:35 p.m. Strangely, I felt nothing: a complete absence in the place where I expected emotion to come storming in.

In the hallway Dr. Loyola stared at the ceiling. "That was tough," he said. "Was that your first . . ."

"Yeah," I said, numb. I kept waiting for sadness or some emotion to hit me. I watched the nurses scurry up and down the unit.

"You go home and get some sleep," he said.

"Yes, sir," I said, moving mechanically toward the hospital doors. As I walked through the parking lot, I felt like a child's toy that had been wound up and set in motion, wholly divorced from my body.

I got in the same car I'd driven since my undergrad days at FSU, started the engine, and pulled onto the I-95 South, heading for Jupiter. Only a few pairs of headlights streamed down the freeway at this late hour. Suddenly, I had a vision from my past. I recalled, with incredible intensity, the waitress who had served me late-night breakfast at Denny's all those years ago in San Francisco. The image of her standing on her feet, alone, late into the night coalesced with the image of my patient dying without any family by her bedside. I knew neither of these women's stories. I had spoken only a few words to the waitress; I hadn't spoken to my patient before she had been intubated. I didn't know their families. I didn't know what God, if any, they worshiped. But I felt them. The lonely pain these two women shared coursed through my soul.

Finally, I cried. I cried the whole way back to Jupiter.

The next morning, when I had gotten my emotions in check, I called Daddy. I hadn't wanted to talk to him while I was bawling. Neurosurgery is a high-risk medical specialty; death is inevitable. What if he thought I couldn't handle the emotional toll? But I needed to talk through the experience of losing a patient for the first time. Daddy remained silent until I had said my piece.

"You're going into the right profession, Myron."

I had expected him to tell me to toughen up, bite the bullet, and get back in the OR. "Oh?" I asked.

"You know why?"

"Why, Daddy?"

"You care. You cared about that woman, and you care about your patients."

My resolve to maintain a steely stoicism went right out the window. "You just said a word, Daddy," I told him, fresh tears rolling down my cheeks.

"Now," he said, "it's already eight a.m. Why aren't you at the hospital?"

A laugh choked through my tears. Daddy was back to shooting bullets. I wouldn't have wanted it any other way. We Rolles don't mind a good cry. But we always wipe our tears and get back to work.

How I responded to losing a patient was a pivotal moment in my development as a physician. As I moved through my final year of medical school, I had the confidence that I had chosen the right profession. That confidence allowed me to branch out during my away rotations.

In my final year, I traveled to Cedars-Sinai, the University of Pittsburgh, the Mayo Clinic, and the University of Miami to do rotations with neurosurgeons. During these rotations, I'd function as a de facto resident: a doctor in training who practices medicine under the supervision of a senior doctor known as an attending physician. I would wrench 2 percent out of experts who knew what it took to succeed.

During my visitation at Cedars-Sinai, I worked with doctors who practiced at UCLA in Los Angeles, recognized for consecutive years as one of the top neurosurgery programs in the nation. I wanted to learn from the best and brightest. I was allowed to observe an operation on a lumbar disc herniation. I stood side by side with a second-year orthopedic surgery resident. The attending performing the surgery asked us questions, testing our knowledge of the procedure in real time. It was clear that the second-year resident was struggling. He either didn't prepare or didn't know much about the spine.

At one point the attending asked us, "What is this?" As a fourth-year medical student, not even an MD, I had been respectfully deferring to the second-year, but he was tongue-tied. I couldn't resist.

"That's the yellow ligament. *Ligamentum flavum.* That's right before you get to the thecal sac."

The attending paused to look up at me, his eyes lighting up. "Very good," he said.

All the work I put in—2 percent at a time—gave me the knowledge to answer that question. I was proud of myself. I knew I'd be able to make it in a neurosurgery residency. The orthopedic resident never talked to me after that.

Next up: the University of Pittsburgh. Their away rotation offered me the chance to work with famous neurosurgeons, including the team doctor for the Pittsburgh Steelers. In the operating room, the residents of Pittsburgh were impressed with my ability to sew and suture. They asked me, "Where did you learn how to use a needle like that?"

"In my apartment," I replied. "I practiced a lot on my own."

But it wasn't all smooth sailing at Pittsburgh. You've probably seen medical programs on television where a senior physician walks through rounds quizzing interns. It's real—and stressful. We had to be on our A-game continually because we never knew when questions would be machine-gunned our way. One afternoon, a handful of residents, the attending, and I were walking through the hospital.

"Myron, tell me about a Chiari malformation," the attending quizzed.

I remembered reading about this condition. But the information wouldn't come to the tip of my tongue. I couldn't remember what it was, how it formed, or who it afflicted.

The attending smelled blood. Some doctors can be like sharks that way—once there is a little chum in the water, they pick you apart. "What's a Chiari II?" he continued. "What symptoms are associated with a Chiari II malformation?"

"I . . ."

"What's a Chiari III? What's associated with a Chiari III malformation?"

"I don't know," I said.

He knew I didn't know, but he was proving a point. "Well, let me explain," he said. "A Chiari is a condition in which brain tissue extends into your spinal canal. It occurs when part of your skull is abnormally small or misshapen, pressing on your brain and forcing it downward."

I had been caught off guard, unprepared. I took it as a challenge. I went home from the hospital, and I read about where the name Chiari came from. I watched videos on Chiari operations, including a suboccipital craniectomy with a C1 laminectomy. By the end of the night, there was no question about a Chiari for which I did not have a rapid-fire answer.

Then I thought, "He's probably not going to ask me about

Chiari's again. He expects you to know that now, right? He'll ask you about patients with other pathologies on our list that we're rounding on."

I found the list of our patients and studied their pathologies. One of the patients had a meningioma, a typical extra-axial lesion—a brain tumor. We had about three or four meningioma patients on our list, and he hadn't asked anyone about meningiomas yet, so I said to myself, "Let me grab two percent on this." It was nearing midnight, but I cracked the textbooks on meningiomas. I learned that they usually occur in middle-aged women. They are benign unless they are anaplastic. Eight out of ten times, the tumor can be removed and the patient lives a full life.

I didn't stop there; my attending's line of questioning could extend into the lesser-known areas. "Let me grab two percent more on what meningiomas are, where they grow, and how to resect them," I told myself. "What does it mean if I resect ten percent of it? What does it mean if I resect the whole meningioma plus the dural tail, plus the bone? What does it mean if I just resect the meningioma without the dural tail, without the bone? What does that mean for recurrence?" I became a meningioma expert.

The next day, I was with the same group doing rounds. I sensed a quiz coming, and sure enough, the attending's voice rang in my ears. "Myron, tell me about the Simpson grades of meningiomas."

Boom. I had predicted the play and was in the perfect position. I even gave him extra information from the literature that I'd read the night before.

"You got that one," he said. Then he upped the ante: "Tell me, if you have any of the superior sagittal sinus, how much of it are you able to take?"

"You're able to take the first one-third of the anterior part of the superior sagittal sinus."

"Not bad."

The attending looked at me and gave me a wink. That wink said:

You were unprepared yesterday, but I see you've fixed that today.
Exactly what the 2% Way enables you to achieve.

● ● ●

The next move in my climb was to be accepted into a residency program: postgraduate training for freshly minted physicians. I applied
to one hundred neurosurgery programs and was accepted into thirty.
Being accepted into a residency doesn't necessarily mean that's where
you'll train. Applicants and the program directors numerically rank
each other in a computer system that uses an algorithm to match
them up. Neither applicants nor the program directors can see how
they're being ranked by the other party. If I ranked Penn number
one and they ranked me number one, I'd be headed to Penn. But if
I ranked Penn number one and they ranked me number thirty-four,
then I would have to settle for a choice further down the line.

My choices needed to be intentional: neurosurgery residencies
are seven years long. If the program wasn't a good fit, my career
and my future ability to impact global health would suffer. Most
of the programs would offer state-of-the-art equipment and staff
with all manner of awards. I wanted something more, two things
specifically: community and vision.

I'm a community guy. I believe in the power of prayer and the
power of loved ones. Community, family, and God are my energy
sources. They drive me forward. Sometimes I just need somebody I
trust to tell me that it's going to be okay. I need to hear, "We've got
you." Those are not only words; my support systems are my anchor.
Serving my community gives my life purpose. My family is my rock,
my foundation. The Lord is my shepherd; he is always with me. I
am never truly alone if I have community, family, and faith. I was
looking for these qualities in a medical center. I wanted to belong to
a medical group of like-minded individuals.

Vision was also vital. I'd devoted a lot of my life to the grind of football and medical school. When I'm grinding, I put my shoulder to the wheel and start pushing. There are no shortcuts: it's grind, grind, grind. Now that I'd moved on from that grind, what was next? I needed to look down the road to the next seven years and beyond. I wanted to learn in an institution that would share my vision of service to underserved communities. I knew there was something more significant for me out there, and I wanted a residency that would join me in my vision. I wasn't going into medicine to get rich; my vision was to enrich the lives of others.

I devised a strategy that allowed me to look deeper. This focus is important when facing a massive decision. You need to look down to the core. What do you want to define your experience? When I toured facilities, I watched the way the residents spoke to one another. I wouldn't speak or ask questions; I'd just observe their interpersonal interactions. I'd watch for clues about the residents' day-to-day lives. Did they know each other? Did they seem healthy? Did they have some bond, something that connected them besides ambition?

At several of the programs I toured, the residents looked run-down. Their hair was unwashed, their white coats were crinkled, and their shoes looked crusty. They snapped at one another and seemed nervous when the attendings came into the room.

When I visited Massachusetts General Hospital, where Harvard trains its residents, I was blown away. At Mass General, I saw residents laughing with each other and teasing each other. "This reminds me of football," I thought. "This reminds me of the camaraderie of the locker room."

The Mass General residents looked cohesive. That came from the top down. Harvard's chairman, Dr. Bob Carter, took me aside and told me his vision for residents: "I'm looking to find tomorrow's leaders in neurosurgery, people who will change neurosurgery in their own unique way." The warm rush of certainty flowed through my veins.

I didn't have to be a carbon copy of everyone else who went to Mass General and did molecular biogenetic research or immuno-chemical research or some type of nanotechnology research. Dr. Carter encouraged me to find my own purpose, to pursue my own vision. I already knew I wanted to combine pediatric neurosurgery with global health. I wanted to care for the marginalized and less fortunate individuals in America and around the world, especially in Black and Brown populations.

When I submitted my rankings, Harvard was top of the list.

1. Harvard University
2. University of Pennsylvania
3. Vanderbilt University
4. University of Miami
5. University of Pittsburgh

Now all I could do was wait for match day. In medical school, match day is a bigger event than graduation. Students receive a single letter with their residency decision—and their future—tucked inside.

That day, all sixty of Florida State University's fourth-year medical students and their families crowded into a large auditorium. My close friend Makini Thompson, Cory, Mummy, and Daddy were by my side as I walked in and received my letter, sealed in a large brown envelope. Giant golden balloons spelling out MATCH DAY adorned the stage. It reminded me of a miniature version of the NFL draft. Our fates were encased in those plain brown envelopes. Both tears of joy and disappointment would be shed.

That day was my second draft—a chance at redemption in the second act. I reflected on the disappointment I had experienced during the 2010 NFL Draft. Not today: today I would hear Massachusetts General call my name.

Our dean took the stage. "You've done so well. You've come so far," he told the crowd. "This is the moment you've all been waiting for. Stand up and open your letters."

I rose and tore the edge off my envelope. A sheet of white paper fell out.

Congratulations, you are matched to Massachusetts General Hospital.

I handed the letter to Mummy, who yelped with joy. She gave it to Daddy, who nodded stoically. I hugged Cory, feeling my brother's arm wrap around me.

Students started going onstage with their families, announcing their choice.

"Mummy, I want you to read my letter to everyone," I told her.

"Myron, I hate public speaking," she said, embarrassed.

"Mummy, practice saying, 'My son Myron Rolle will do his residency in neurosurgery at Harvard, Massachusetts General Hospital.'"

She looked doubtful.

"Just say that over and over again while we wait."

That helped settle her nerves and gave her a goal she could focus on. Yet when we walked up on stage, Mummy tried to give me the slip. "Myron, can't you just say it? I'm nervous."

"No, Mummy," I said, giddy with joy. "I want you to do it."

When my turn came, we Rolles marched up to the podium. I never got to walk onstage and hug the commissioner in the NFL draft. Now I was about to do something just as meaningful and fulfilling—and my parents would share the moment with me.

As Daddy gave a quick speech, I remembered back to the day in the stands in Galloway when I lay back in Daddy's embrace, wanting to play football like my older brother so I could bask in the warmth of my father's approval. The same warm rush of love and approval enveloped me now. Daddy couldn't shout out loud as he had for Whitney on the football field, but the same vibrations echoed through me like he was yelling from the mountaintops. He's been the rock under my feet since I could walk. "Now Myron's mother is going to announce where he's going," Daddy concluded.

Mummy opened the letter and spoke in a pitch-perfect voice, "Myron is going to do his neurosurgery residency at Harvard, Massachusetts General Hospital." The crowd went nuts.

She started smiling, relieved, and I hugged her. "Wonderful job, Mummy," I said.

Walking off the stage, I thanked God. We can't know his plan, but we must trust it. Blessing often comes in the guise of tragedy. My unrealized dream of becoming a first-round NFL draft pick became the blessing that led me to this moment.

The book of Isaiah states, "Fear not, for I am with you; be not dismayed, for I am your God; I will strengthen you, I will help you, I will uphold you with my righteous right hand" (Isaiah 41:10 ESV). His righteous hand guided me to Harvard and Mass General. His righteous hand safeguarded me from banging my head over and over again in the NFL, preserving me from the brain damage inflicted on many of my peers. His righteous hand protected my hands so I can perform the most delicate brain surgeries. His righteous hand has strengthened and upheld me.

● ● ●

I didn't know much about Boston before I moved there. "It's cold and racist" was the half-joking response I got from most Black people I talked to. I moved into a studio apartment on the seventeenth floor of a thirty-nine-floor high-rise connected to the TD Garden, where the Celtics and Bruins play. My windows looked out to the Zakim Bridge.

I chose the place because it was a four-minute walk from the hospital. I could wake up at 5:50 a.m., get to the hospital at 5:54 a.m. and be ready for rounds at 6:00.

The first thing I sought out in Boston was a barbershop in a

Black neighborhood. I found one in Roxbury, where Bobby Brown and New Edition hailed from. A bunch of Jamaican guys ran the place. They called me Doc because every time I shaped up there, I wore scrubs.

My other necessity was a church. Every Sunday, I took an Uber to Mattapan, a rough part of the city, to attend Morning Star Baptist, a Black megachurch. In my first days in the city, when I felt isolated from my home, the pastor, Bishop John Borders, and I became close. We sat courtside for a Celtics game against the 76ers. And he invited me over to his house, where I met his family.

I needed those support systems in place as I started my residency. I've spoken a lot in this book about forging my own identity in a space where others tried to superimpose their ideas on me. The first days of my residency at Massachusetts General Hospital were no different. I entered a place that hasn't typically seen someone who looks like me walk through its doors: not only Black but also an established figure in my own right.

First-year residents are at the bottom of the totem pole. Most of my peers were newly out of school, and I had already lived a life filled with experiences they would never have. The *Washington Post* came to my match day. (Ironically, I finally got my media event for my commitment announcement, which the Hun School had denied me all those years ago.) Shortly after I arrived in Boston, I did an interview on CNN with Sanjay Gupta, a neurosurgeon from Emory. "You are a high-profile resident coming in. Do you think you're going to have to perform at a higher level?" he asked.

I'd answered in the affirmative. "I do think I'll have to perform at higher levels," I said. "But one thing I've always been is prepared. When they call my number, I'll be ready to go, ready to learn."[1]

No matter how careful I was with my words in interviews, the public attention created an unprecedented dynamic between me, the chief resident, and the other residents. Some of them thought I would come in with sunglasses on and a "can't tell me nothing" attitude because I was *the* Myron Rolle. Reporters at the hospital doors asked me, "How are you going to be able to take orders from someone younger than you when you've played in the NFL?"

Once again I had to break a misconception of my identity. Doing so wasn't a burden, and it didn't overwhelm me. When you know your enemy is coming—in this case the enemy being a label or any form of stereotype—you can deal with it.

I dealt with it by being a hungry rookie again. I hit my assignments hard. I stumbled at times. I made my share of mistakes, just like any junior resident. But I tried to correct my mistakes quickly, and I unabashedly asked for help often, which is antithetical to the cocky label some people placed on me.

Still, I heard murmurs. One senior resident let me know the score one day after rounds. "You have a reputation of thinking you are above it all," he said.

"That's not who I am," I told him.

"I know that. But you'll have to show them," the resident said.

I'd been a rookie before. And I was prepared to be one again. I know what it takes to buy into a hierarchical structure. I told my fellow residents, "I'm a team player. You can ask my teammates." Time would tell if they'd believe me.

Community was hard to come by among my fellow residents. So, like many other times in my life, I found that community in the company of a Black woman. Imani McElroy was a general surgery resident. In our first year, we were going through similar experiences. That's not to say she came in with a reputation, but she did come in as a Black woman with natural hair. She was from the Bay Area of California and looked different from everyone else in her program.

Black and Brown women are my champions, my heroes, my cowarriors. We fight together. They're honest with me; they're real with me. That began with my mother. She set the example of what a strong Black woman should be. I had seen those same qualities in Bridgette and in Aisha, and now I saw them in Imani.

Imani and I sat and drank tea together after rounds. We went to a Red Sox game at Fenway Park. We grabbed food together after work. We communicated via text on some of the challenges and struggles in our respective programs. It was a blessing to have somebody like her to bounce ideas off of and laugh with through some of our trials and tribulations. She was my teammate that first year. We fought together, like warriors. Instead of pads and uniforms, we were clad for battle in scrubs.

Imani's support was invaluable; Harvard Medical wasn't going to be easy. All neurosurgery residencies are challenging. And a top-notch program like Harvard at Massachusetts General ratchets up that difficulty to another level. In football, it was like going from college to pro. Mass General doesn't refer patients to other hospitals; other hospitals send their toughest cases to us. No one goes anywhere after Mass General. We're the backstop, the last line of defense. In that way, it's a lot like being a safety; there's no one behind you. It's you or the great beyond.

As with Oxford professors and NFL coaches, Harvard Medical attendings expected their new residents to do incredibly well from the get-go. Everyone I spoke to and interacted with was an expert in their field. They held you to the same high standard to which they held themselves.

I had an advantage. None of the other incoming residents had played professional football. Residents must commit volumes of information to memory to be pulled up in the heat of the moment. For this, football had prepared me well. I had memorized hundreds of playbooks, information I had to retrieve in tenths of a second as I ran at top speed while covering receivers who were world-class sprinters. Attending physicians demanded students know complex cases inside out and to prepare for any potentiality. It was similar to game prep at FSU. What was the coverage if the opposing team ran one of the dozens of pass plays in its arsenal? What if they ran it in a shotgun formation or rolled right? How would my responsibilities change if they overloaded one side of the field? Attendings expected us to be prepared in the same way. What happens if the patient does X, Y, or Z? What all could go wrong, and how would I remedy each scenario in seconds?

The lessons I had learned on the football field prepared me mentally, physically, emotionally, and spiritually for the long hours and challenges that lay ahead. I knew it was going to be tough. But I had always tackled every challenge head-on. I knew what hard work looked like. I had risen early and dedicated myself to improving 2 percent every day for years on the biggest stages: Florida State football, the Rhodes Scholarship, Oxford, the NFL, FSU medical school, and now Harvard Medical School at Massachusetts General. Welcome to the league, Dr. Rolle.

My first assignment at Mass General was a general surgery rotation. Gallbladder removals, exams with a patient under anesthesia, and colostomies filled my schedule. These procedures required expertise in suturing, tying wounds closed, and two-handed proficiency with scalpel and forceps. "No sweat," I thought. I'd mastered these techniques in medical school.

One of my first general surgery cases required removal of a patient's thyroid gland, a butterfly-shaped organ in the base of your neck that releases the hormones that control the metabolic system. The extraction went smoothly, and the attending physician asked me to suture and tie the wound. I struggled with the needle as I threaded the stitches through the skin of the neck. My movements were imprecise. I realized, with the bright lights of the OR burning down on me, that I was out of practice. It had been a long time since I'd sat tying shoelaces around strips of rubber.

The attending asked point-blank, "How much have you been practicing?"

"Every other day," I answered.

"Okay," he said, and took over.

His monosyllabic reply spoke volumes. When attendings don't

feel that a resident has the capacity to suture and tie, they don't allow you to do anything else during the case. They can't trust you. If your knots aren't tight, you run the risk of the wound breaking open. Blood can rush in, contaminate the space, and cause infection. I needed to perfect my fundamentals before I could progress.

Once again I relied on the 2% Way, which allowed me to focus on my progress rather than my deficiencies. I'd heard about a senior general surgery resident named Dan Hashimoto who ran a skills lab in the evenings. I emailed Dan, explaining that I had another thyroid surgery scheduled in three weeks and struggled with the procedure.

When my shift ended at six o'clock, I headed directly to the skills lab where I'd practice with Dr. Hashimoto for two hours. It was like grinding with a teammate after practice. We connected over both being immigrants: Dr. Hashimoto is of Japanese descent but grew up in South America and speaks fluent Japanese and Spanish.

Dr. Hashimoto was as demanding as any of my coaches at FSU or Tennessee. He would give me different materials and make me stitch them together. I sutured pieces of foam together: 2 percent better. I tied together parts of animal legs and more delicate things like little pieces of film: 2 percent more proficient. I sutured beneath a microscope and in awkward positions: 2 percent more technical. I used my left hand and my right hand: 2 percent more ambidextrous. Dan made me stitch down inside deep holes where I couldn't see well, but my knots needed to be perfect: 2 percent more confident.

I practiced in the few idle moments I had in my day, and my confidence grew with my skills. I prepared for cases by looking at CT scans and MRIs over and over again as if I were watching game tape. I read studies and medical journals as I had read my playbook, alone in my room at night. I played out every scenario in the OR just as I had on the football field.

In three weeks, when I went into a thyroid case with the attending physician, I was Mass General prepared. It showed. I stitched sutures with speed and confidence; my knots were tight.

"What have you been doing?" the attending asked.

"Dr. Hashimoto has been taking me under his wing every day for the last three weeks," I said as the patient was wheeled away to the recovery room.

The next thing you know, everyone in the department praised Dan as a mentor, a leader. That's one of the beautiful aspects of the 2% Way: you acknowledge the people who've helped you to become the most realized version of yourself. I thank the Lord that he has placed these people in my path. They have helped me become the man I am today. I owe a 2 percent debt to many people in my life, and I hope to pay it back one day with 2 percent interest.

"Perfect sutures in my thyroid procedure," I texted Imani.

"Go get 'em, Dr. Rolle," she messaged back. "Let's have tea tomorrow. A lot to talk about."

As I grew in my abilities as a neurosurgeon, I wanted to replace the identity of the cocky upstart that had been thrown at me. Like any rookie on a football team, I wanted to let my performance do the talking. Over tea, Imani helped me realize that my identity didn't come from a shift in behavior as much as a shift in mindset.

"Society paints a picture of you, to which they expect you to conform," she said. "But you have no control over what others think."

"I know the attending physicians feel good about my work, and they trust me with their patients. My patients have good outcomes," I said. "So what if I walk tall with a bit of swagger?"

"I respect the way you walk into a room," Imani said. "If you changed the way you hold yourself to impress some surgical residents, I'd be questioning you."

As a younger man, I would have asked, "Why aren't these people giving me the respect I deserve? I've earned my place here." As a mature man, I'd found my path and was talking through my actions. Time in and time out, I got the job done and did it well. If that changed other residents' preconceptions of me, fine. If it didn't, that's a *them* problem, not a *me* problem. I decided that day to stop trying to change people's opinions. I was focused on one thing and one thing only: being the best neurosurgeon I could be. I owed that to my patients.

Whenever I was frustrated, I thought about the first patient I had lost, the woman who had died without her family by her side at St. Lucie Medical Center. The image of her coding in that lonely hospital bed often came to mind, and when it did, I heard Daddy's voice in my ears. "Myron, you're going into the right profession."

Mine had been the last hand she held before she slipped into the next world. Just as my life had once belonged to my parents' sacrifice, it now belonged to my patients. I needed to be 2 percent better for them with every movement of my scalpel. I promised my life to my patients and in doing so found the motivation I needed to survive Harvard Medical School.

Chapter 9

FOR ONCE IN MY LIFE

The winter of my third year as a Harvard resident was bitterly cold. When I ran along the banks of the frozen Charles River, my earbuds pumped Southern rap, a reminder of the warmer climates of my past.

I spent my weekends at Mass General. On a Saturday in January, Boston was blanketed in white after an overnight snowstorm. The senior resident, another junior resident, and I were the only neurosurgical staff at the hospital. Dr. William Curry, a Black attending who took a liking to me, allowed his residents more autonomy on weekend shifts. Attendings let us run the unit until an operative case presented itself or a highly challenging patient workup required more experienced insight.

I relished the freedom. Two years of incremental improvements had given me the confidence to tackle whatever challenge came through the doors. Icy roads often led to increased head trauma cases resulting from car accidents and slip-and-falls. So as the hard winter set in weeks before, I had mentally prepared myself for these trauma cases that were often life-threatening. But what walked into the hospital that day was a dramatically different kind of trauma—a trauma that I would share alongside the patient.

In the late afternoon, we admitted a man who'd just had his first seizure at age fifty. Seizures that late in life demand a full brain-imaging workup. The man's MRI showed a lesion on his left temporal lobe. The temporal lobe is one of the more epileptogenic parts of the brain. Any irritation of its tissue, whether from a vascular malformation, a tumor, or a cyst, can cause dangerous, frequent seizures.

I led the surgical team that would perform an immediate lesionectomy. The lesion had formed close to the brain's surface, so we wouldn't have to dig deep through healthy tissue. We could remove the problem while keeping the temporal lobe intact.

I visited the room of the patient, whom I'll refer to as Ben. He lay in bed, tended by a nurse we will call Denise. Three burly guys stood in the corner of the room. They looked like they moved heavy things bare-handed for a living.

"Hey, doc," Ben greeted me in his thick Boston accent.

I introduced myself and began the preoperative consultation. I take great care with this part of my job. All patients deserve to hear an honest assessment of what they're facing so that they can give formal, informed consent. As I explained to Ben that he would undergo a routine lesionectomy, I could tell that he was fraught with fear. I felt duty-bound to make him feel as safe and comfortable as possible, so I took an extra thirty minutes to walk him through the procedure.

"We're going to position you on your back and turn your head to the right," I told him. "We're going to bring our Brainlab machine right over the top of your head. It'll give us laser-sharp focus on the location of the lesion. How does that sound?"

He nodded. Men of his age are often stoically quiet, a demeanor that can belie anxiety, panic, and terror.

"We've done this procedure many times. But there are risks. We'll give you antibiotics to help mitigate infections that could arise. And there's a risk of bleeding. There are many important arteries and veins in the area that we do our very best to avoid. The Brainlab system is an immense help in that. It's like an extremely accurate

GPS that will guide us around your brain. I want you to understand that we're working in an area that is very seizure fertile. Frankly, manipulating any part of the brain can cause seizures postoperatively, so you'll need to take anti-seizure medications."

Ben nodded and relaxed his body. I could tell he was at least slightly reassured. Next came the most difficult part of our conversation, the part patients and families dread. I carefully explained the risk of stroke, coma, and death. "It rarely happens," I said. "But everyone needs to know this: what we're about to undertake together is no trivial thing. *If* there are complications, who would you like me to call?"

"My brother," Ben said. He nodded to one of the large men in the corner of the room who wore a heavy flannel jacket. The brother grunted.

"The whole process should take about six hours," I said to the brother. Preoperative consultations are just as much for the family as they are for the patient. I wanted the brother to know when he could expect Ben to wake up so he wouldn't worry unnecessarily.

"Thank you, Dr. Rolle. I understand," Ben said.

"You're in good hands," I said.

At that moment, I heard one of the men in the corner snicker. Then the brother said, "I can't believe they are going to let a n——operate on Ben." He spoke the slur boldly, as if I weren't in the room.

Denise, a white woman, took a step back from Ben's bed. We caught eyes, her brow furrowing in offense. "I'm sorry," she mouthed.

Strangely, my initial reaction wasn't anger. For the first few moments after the brother spoke, my indignation was entirely professional. I was one of only three neurosurgeons stretched thin over a massive hospital on a busy day. My time was too valuable to waste on this guy.

Then my synapses fired. *He isn't rude, he just called you a . . .*

An old anger, hot and deep-seated, roared through my chest. It was an anger I thought I'd left behind years ago, but I could feel a young Myron Rolle itching to take hold of my body. It was the Myron who fought that boy on the school bus in Galloway after he called me a n—— and said my mummy was a b——. "*Lay your hands on these boys,*" that Myron whispered, tempting me. My heart rate spiked. *Boom, boom, boom.* Young Myron had taken control of my heart and was trying to ready the rest of my body for the fight he wanted.

I lowered my head—not in submission but defiance. I closed my eyes, calmed my breathing, and willed the older, self-possessed Myron to reemerge. After a few seconds, I was once again in full control of my faculties. Still, the brother's words reverberated in my head. So, in my mind, I responded to those words with the assertive voice I'd worked hard to nurture: "*I am here at this moment for a purpose—to save your brother's life. You are trying to test me by halting this moment. But I am going to push through and fulfill my purpose.*"

I lifted my head and gazed at Ben. He looked at me with confused but attentive eyes, almost the same expression he'd had as I explained his operation minutes before. I couldn't determine whether he was distressed by his brother or simply preoccupied with the brain surgery he was about to endure. As I tried to read Ben's face, I realized, "*Wait a minute, I still have to operate on this man's brain.*"

My next step was simple—get out of the room as fast as possible with the consent process concluded. I quickly marked Ben's right ear with a permanent marker so the anesthesiologist would know which side we'd operate on. Ben signed the consent forms without hesitation. "I have to go now. I'll see you down there," I said and jetted toward the door. The three men stood motionless as I moved past them. "*Head up. Eyes forward. Don't look at his brother.*" I'd given this family my Hippocratic oath, but I owed them not one more second of my time.

I jetted to the hospital cafeteria and inhaled a sports drink. Away from the situation, I could focus my full mind on pushing younger Myron out of my body. The last bit of liquid disappeared down my throat, and young Myron vanished along with it. I stood up and went back to the counter and bought two more bottles. It was going to be a long day. I needed vitality, not vitriol.

The brother might have thought that his words would shock me or jar me into a confrontation. He didn't know I'd seen this play before and knew every move. I knew this scenario was bound to happen when I packed up and moved to Boston, a segregated city, so I practiced my defensive moves many times in my head. On the field, when my opponent was reckless—and stupid—I was there to intercept the ball and take back control of the game. The same goes for confronting racism. My goal is to shut down the attack in my mind and play the scene on *my* terms.

Even when my opponent is unexceptional, I refuse to let my efforts drop. When walking around Mass General in my scrubs, I often encountered casual and unconscious racism. A father thought I was a janitor and asked me to clean up his ailing daughter's spilled juice. A mother in the cafeteria tried to hand me a twenty-dollar bill, misidentifying me for a cashier. Once when I walked into a patient's room, he waved dismissively at his lunch tray, saying, "Take it, I'm done." These types of incidents carry a racial undertone that I, as a Black doctor, feel palpably when I'm trying to do my job. This day, those undertones rose in volume and became painful, racist noise.

I'd controlled myself in Ben's room, but I still had a choice to make. My colleagues would be completely understanding if I asked to be relieved of my patient, and it was within my rights to have another doctor scrub in for me. Unsure of the path I'd take, I wanted to talk to someone who could truly empathize with my position—someone Black. I found an empty office, closed the door, and called Dr. Curry.

"I'm a little shook right now," I said after explaining the situation. "When I encounter racism, it's often ignorant and unconscious. I haven't faced this kind of blatant bigotry in ages."

"When's the last time someone called you that word?" Dr. Curry asked.

"To my face? When I was a kid in New Jersey. On a school bus."

"And what happened that day?"

"I ended up in court."

"Myron, you're a far cry from that kid in Galloway. You're a trained, professional physician. You acted like one in that room."

Dr. Curry asked me about the patient and the other men. "They looked like they worked in a steel mill," I said. "They were big, almost linebacker-big."

"He was speaking from ignorance," said Dr. Curry astutely.

"In Boston these people seem much more out in the open. In other places, like Florida State or the cities I'd travel to while in the NFL, the racism felt more covert. Maybe it was there, but I was shielded from it to an extent because I was a known football player. And it's impossible to make out the words of a single fan when on the field in those stadiums. You'd never know the difference between a racial slur and a cheer."

"I don't think Boston has more racist people than other cities. In my experience, I've realized that some people, like the ones you dealt with today, feel emboldened by the circumstances," Dr. Curry said. "They could see that, essentially, you were their servant at that moment. They aren't wrong in that regard; a good doctor is there to serve anyone in need. But that dynamic can give some people a false sense of ownership. And we live in a country where ownership of someone else is tied to racism, epithets, and divisive language. Hateful words are bound to bubble up. It may be inevitable, but as Black men, we don't have to engage with it. You have no obligation to operate on this patient."

"I understand," I said. "Thank you. But I'm going to do it."

"Are you sure?"

"How often does someone have the chance to change a racist's assumptions? If I walk away, I do nothing but let that man off the hook. But if I operate, I will force him to confront himself. When my patient wakes up in the ICU, successfully operated on and seizure-free, his brother will know—even if he won't admit it—that it was a Black man who helped save his brother's life. He may not say thank you out loud, but somewhere inside, he will feel gratitude."

"That's a nice thought, Myron. But I think you know as well as I do that that likely won't be his reaction. People don't often change in an instant. His are deeply felt beliefs, and hate can be too entrenched to dislodge."

Dr. Curry was right. I could complete a perfect brain operation on Ben, and his brother could still call me a slur as he left the hospital. So I changed my perspective. There was still something to gain from this ugly situation—practice and experience. If this surgery increased my skill set by 2 percent, I'd have something to show for this ordeal.

"Well, then frankly, Dr. Curry, I have a job to do. I want those surgical hours."

"Spoken like a true junior resident," Dr. Curry said. "Let me know how the procedure goes alongside your attending of record."

"Thank you," I said. "I'm ready to operate."

Dr. Curry didn't tell me what to do. He made no assumptions about my mindset, and he didn't tell me my feelings were wrong. He simply listened, giving me the freedom to make up my own mind. In speaking with him in such an honest way, I began to see how I could channel his approach to guide others confronted with similar situations. On a more immediate level, his leadership ensured that I regained the necessary frame of mind to get my job done.

I scrubbed up and went into the operating room, focused on my job. We needed to take out the "offending agent" placing pressure on the vital parts of his brain. (The irony was not lost on me.) We also needed to relieve pressure on the cranium and do a biopsy on the tumor.

I used a drill to take off the bone, preserving that part of Ben's skull in a sterile solution so it would be aseptic when I reattached it at the end of the procedure. When I excised the dura, the outside covering of the brain, I did so delicately, careful to preserve its integrity so that it could be reconnected.

With Ben's head open and exposed, I was afforded a rare opportunity: I had a direct view into the brain of someone who likely hated me because of the color of my skin. Of course, I wasn't expecting his brain to look any different from the other brains I'd operated on. It was pink, no different from yours and mine. As I examined Ben's brain, I couldn't help but remember, just for a moment, the incident in his hospital room. Suddenly, I felt a profound sense of serenity. I realized I had a single role to play in my work as a neurosurgeon, centered on one task. That task was clear and simple: there are brains that need help, and I could administer that treatment.

After burning the surface of the brain called the pial layer, I put my fingers into a pair of microscissors and adroitly cut through it. With an electrocautery, an instrument used to spread and burn tissue, I found a corridor that led straight to the dark lesion sitting less than a centimeter deep in Ben's brain. The lesion's margins extended to the posterior, anterior, lateral, and medial. I removed a small piece to be sent to pathology, then cut around the lesion's edges. As I removed the lesion *en bloc*, which means as one single piece, I couldn't help but smile at my work. There was no bleeding into the operative site and no bleeding in the cavity left by the tumor. We got to hemostasis, put a thrombotic agent in the cavity to keep it clean of blood, closed the dura, and sealed it watertight.

Once my attending and I scrubbed out, I called Dr. Curry again. "We removed the lesion *en bloc*," I told him. "Patient is stable in the ICU."

"I'm proud of the way you handled yourself," he said. "How did you feel during the procedure?"

"I focused on the task at hand and gained a sense of clarity."

"I've felt that during surgery. I know how important that moment can be. Live with that moment for a little bit."

Over the course of one frigid day in January, I'd flipped an ugly situation on its head. My surgical skills improved, and after following up on Ben's recuperation, I learned that a postoperative MRI showed we'd completely removed his lesion. I got 2 percent better at compartmentalizing my emotions when on the job, a vital bit of emotional control that surgery necessitates. I was 2 percent better at understanding the pathological nature of racism. It was a disease to be removed, and I was developing the skills to take out the lesion and return others' brains to the beautiful, complex organs God has given us.

The only way to tackle racism is through systemic change. That change has to come from places with resources. Harvard Medical has made steps toward racial justice since that day. The killings of George Floyd and Breonna Taylor in the summer of 2020 forced the staff to have long-overdue conversations. Harvard provided funding for racial justice efforts at the hospital, centering Black voices.

In addition, Dr. Curry established a consortium of Black residents and doctors at Mass General. Over a series of Zoom meetings, the fifty or so participants of the consortium spoke honestly about their emotions as Black medical practitioners in Boston. As a member of the consortium, I listened to each of my colleagues with an open heart and mind. Over the course of several meetings, I found we all had many overlapping frustrations.

But Black people are not a monolith. We had differing ideas on how to address those frustrations. Sometimes I disagreed with many of my peers' positions on how to curb the racial issues we faced.

"I'm tired of teaching white people what they ought to do and say in moments like this," said one resident, echoing a common idea among consortium participants. "We shouldn't have to be spokespeople for the entire Black world, informing white people about whatever it is they want to know about the Black experience."

I understand that frustration. Given the amount of emotional lifting I and many others have done to overcome the effects of racism, I know how exhausting it is to constantly teach others how to respect your humanity. At the same time, I want to tell my Black community that now is not the time to be fatigued. Yes, white people must take on the onus of educating themselves and figuring out solutions to racial inequality. But we can't simply say, "I'm letting this go unchallenged because I'm simply too fed up to take it on."

The terror experienced by the marchers on Selma's Edmund Pettus Bridge could have caused MLK and his movement to retreat in fear and exhaustion. Not only did they not quit, they redoubled their efforts. Too often, as victims of oppression, we feel it's solely the duty of the perpetrator to make things right. But just as a person with cancer must fight tooth and nail against a force that aims to kill them, we, the victims of racism, must work ourselves if we are going to reach the promised land.

This isn't in the least bit fair, of course. Asking the wronged to do most of the heavy lifting to fix the problem is antithetical to our concept of justice. But suppose each of us gives that extra 2 percent of effort toward working to educate white citizens, eradicate racism, and tear down systems of oppression. In that case, I know we can overcome discrepancies of racial privilege and bring the world closer to equality.

● ● ●

There were a few warm moments in that long, brutal Boston winter of 2019. Often after I returned home from an exceptionally long day at Mass General, I'd be standing in my apartment's entrance, shaking off the snow from my shoulders, when my phone would ring. It was always the same person: Dr. Latoya Legrand, who knew exactly when I'd return home from the hospital.

I first came to know Dr. Legrand by reading about her. In September 2018, I was browsing a Black medical professional networking group's website. A profile on a pediatric dentist caught my eye. In her photograph, Dr. Legrand wore blue scrubs and flashed a big, bright smile that jumped through my laptop screen.

Dr. Legrand's story grabbed me. From Columbus, Georgia, she went north to attend Tennessee State University. After completing her undergraduate studies, she spent two years sending out applications to dental schools, most of which were rejected. With every rejection email, she thought more and more about changing her career dreams. But she had a passion for working with children, which kept her reaching for her goals even at her lowest points. Her powerful Christian faith pushed her to study for and take the Dental Admission Test three more times until she perfected her score.

Still, most schools wait-listed her. Only at the eleventh hour did she receive news that she'd been accepted to the University of Tennessee. Her unrivaled determination to succeed defined her time at UT. She graduated in the top of her class and, after three years practicing as a general dentist, was accepted into a pediatric dentistry residency program in Birmingham, Alabama.

"I love working with my hands and changing the perception of the dentist being scary," Dr. Legrand told the interviewer whose profile I read.[1] Through success, she hadn't lost perspective on what was most important: her young patients. "What a comeback story," I thought. "This woman is special."

Dr. Legrand's story stayed with me long after I read her profile. I had to reach out to her. I messaged the site's admin on Facebook, who happily connected us. I messaged Dr. Legrand on Facebook, trying to articulate how inspired I'd been by her story. To my delight, she replied with warm thanks—and her phone number.

We began texting. I was consistently blown away by her intelligence, her quick wit, and her impeccable taste in music. One day she texted me a link to Stevie Wonder's "For Once in My Life." "This will cheer up your cold Boston apartment," she wrote.

Our long text threads soon progressed to phone calls and FaceTime chats. I loved that she sported a natural afro. On nights after we'd both survived long shifts, we'd lie in bed and video chat, sharing our case stories and opening up about our goals, fears, and worries. One evening she elaborated on the reasons why she was so passionate about medicine. "From an early age, I've seen how at-risk children are neglected and cast aside," she said. "I have to help them, whether they are autistic or special needs. Their dental health is so frequently forgotten about."

"My motivation with pediatric neurosurgery comes from that same feeling," I told her, my soul feeling like it had finally found a kindred spirit. "These children are the most vulnerable patients in the neurosurgical population, especially in places like Haiti, Grenada, and Guyana."

As we bonded over our professional overlaps and similar aspirations, we grew emotionally closer by commiserating over our struggle to find love. Latoya had recently gone through a divorce, which inspired me to reflect on why my relationships had never taken flight.

Latoya's insights into the complex nature of her marriage helped me realize that in my younger days I had played the game of love wrong. Throughout my twenties, I'd conformed to societal assumptions and pressures about the type of woman a professional athlete should date. We're supposed to show up to red-carpet events with models, actresses, television journalists, and influencers. I always ran into roadblocks with these types of women. Our values and ideals never aligned. Since I hadn't questioned my own assumption, I was unaware that God had another plan for me.

So I prayed. Not for God to bring me a woman to love but for God to give me the strength and wisdom to decide for myself what I needed in a life partner. Of course, passionate love was the foundation. But just as important was finding someone who inspired me to be better. What kind of woman would motivate me to better serve my patients? What kind of relationship would help me better serve God? This relationship had to be with a woman I admired, a woman who, in her strength, inspired me to be the best man I can be. Prayer made me realize that these were elemental qualities in the relationship

I wanted. And when I asked myself who, if anyone, embodied those qualities, the answer was never in doubt: Latoya Legrand.

Latoya truly cared about others, a compassion that had no connection to self-aggrandizement. Her selfless heart was evident when she helped children. "*I am*," I realized, my heart beginning to thud, "*in love*." Real love.

Prayer changes assumption to intention. I decided to tell Latoya how I felt. I was nervous when I dialed the phone, like a kid asking for a date to prom. "Since I've been a boy, I've been very intentional about my life," I told her.

"Oh, I'm aware," she kidded me.

"But there's one thing I want to be clearer about."

"What's that?"

"I intend to be more than your friend. My intentions are to be serious."

"I feel the same way," she replied.

"You know," I said, "there's a flight from Birmingham that leaves tomorrow morning."

When I picked up Latoya from the airport, I had Stevie Wonder's "For Once in My Life" playing in the car. "Turn it up," she said. "This is our song."

I wanted to court Latoya. Maybe I'm old-school, but I cherished holding doors for her and grabbing the check at dinner. I took her to services at Morning Star Baptist Church. She impressed Bishop Borders with her knowledge of the Word. When she went back to Alabama, we did Bible study together over the phone. God connects people—especially those in love—like nothing else.

"What are the two most important commandments to you?" I asked her one night.

"The Bible says the two strongest commandments are to love thy neighbor and love God."

Latoya followed those commandments with her every action. With each decision, she asked herself, "Would this please God?"

At Mass General, my fellow residents at the hospital noticed that I was giddy all the time. "The kid's in love," Dr. Curry commented when I couldn't stop grinning when we scrubbed up for surgery. "Nobody gets that happy about a craniotomy."

In April the snow had finally gone, and Latoya visited Boston all the time. One night Latoya was putting the finishing touches on her outfit before dinner just as the Uber arrived. As we headed out the door, she stopped me. She took a hard look at me, grabbed me by the lapels, and pulled me in closer.

"I'm looking good. She wants a kiss," I thought.

Latoya peered up at my face for a moment, narrowing her eyes in concentration. "Come to the bathroom," she said. "You've got a little toothpaste in your beard."

Latoya led me to the sink, where she cleaned my beard with a washcloth. Then she put in a little grease, brushed it, and made sure it was straight. "Okay," she said and patted me on my lapels. "Now we're ready to go."

A small thing, perhaps, but my heart filled with comfort. My life had been spent in competitive places: locker rooms full of men and surgical wards where I was expected to lead. I'd never had a woman care for me like that.

At that moment, I realized that this young woman saw me not as a football player with his name in lights but as a human being that she loved. She wanted to protect me by making sure I was always at my best. I was no longer representing only myself; I was representing both of us, a unit.

I was ready to get on one knee right then.

At dinner that night, Latoya seemed to sparkle. "Hey," I said, trying to be casual. "I'm on vacation this December."

"What a coincidence. Me too."

"Bet, let's get married then."

"Okay, bet."

"But that's not my official proposal," I said.

"Oh, I *know* that," she said. "You know I want a real proposal."

In May 2019, I had to speak to a board of Black medical executives in Rancho Bernardo, near San Diego, California, and I invited Latoya. Cory came along as well—I'd need backup. After my speech, I pulled Cory aside and showed him the ring I had stashed in my back pocket.

"You certainly didn't skimp on the diamond," he said. "Good man."

"I'm going to ask her tonight after dinner. You distract her so that I can do what I have to do."

I'd booked the three of us a table at Jake's Del Mar, a seafood joint with big windows overlooking the Pacific Ocean. I was so nervous I could barely finish my salmon.

"Y'all want to walk on the beach?" I asked when the check hit the table.

I led the way down to Powerhouse Beach. The palms rustled with a light wind, and the air tasted like salt. I remembered when Cory and I worked out on the beach in Atlantic City as boys. We'd come a long way since those days.

When we reached a spot where the coast spilled out into view, I gave Cory the signal.

"Latoya, look up," he said. "What do the stars say?"

"I'm a dentist, not an astrologist," she said.

Flustered, Cory pulled out his phone. "Hey, Latoya, can you help me with this?" he asked.

When she bent to look at his phone, I slipped down on one knee.

"There's nothing there," she said, confused. She turned around, saw me with my pants in the sand, and burst out laughing.

"Latoya Legrand, will you marry me?"

She kept laughing.

Girl, you got to say yes, I thought.

"Yes! Of course, yes!"

In the Uber back to Rancho Bernardo, I took control of the

music. Stevie Wonder serenaded us as we cruised down the California coast.

Here's my advice to anyone looking for love: find someone who speaks to what's important to you, that gets you on fire, that lights you up, as opposed to who the world has assumed you should be with. That's how I found my soul mate.

● ● ●

In the final days of August, I watched CNN report that a massive hurricane had formed over the Atlantic Ocean and was heading straight for the Bahamas. Hurricane Dorian was a Category 5 storm, and on September 1 it made landfall on the coast of Grand Bahama. The storm stalled over the island for three days, flooding over 60 percent of the housing. I received phone calls and text messages from loved ones who lost their homes or who hadn't eaten in days because they were trapped in their attics as water levels rose. People saw their neighbors swept away into the ocean by tides stronger than Samson.

Wayne Rolle, my cousin from Exuma, lost his family in the storm. He called me days afterward, saying he was still without power and water. "Today I got to the community washhouse at two a.m. to stand in line for the opening at seven a.m. for my first proper shower in a week," he told me.

Latoya watched me pace a hole in the rug as I watched the coverage. "I can't just sit here in my cushy apartment while my country is washed away," I said.

"This is why you got into medicine," she said. "Go help your people."

I called the president of our hospital, Dr. Peter Slavin. "My countrymen are suffering," I told him. "I need to get involved." Slavin connected me with Dr. Hilarie Cranmer, the head of Mass General's Global Disaster Response and Humanitarian Action. She said, "I've got a team heading to Grand Bahama in two days. We'd love to have you along."

Our team was eight strong: a social worker, a midwife, three nurses, a nurse practitioner, me, and another physician. We arrived nine days after the storm. From the moment I stepped off the plane, I felt the massive scope of the destruction. Lines snaked around each grocery store. Ambulances wailed through the streets. The eastern side of the island took the heaviest damage. There was little infrastructure left to speak of—power and broadband lines had been knocked out.

Once we were on the ground, we teamed up with a nongovernmental organization called International Medical Corps. They had already established connections from the World Health Organization and the Bahamian Ministry of Health, from whom they relayed specific briefings.

They sent us to the High Rock district in East Grand Bahama. The medical clinic there, located on a bluff between the coastal road and the sea, had been destroyed. I stood on what was left of the old clinic: a pile of cinder blocks and twisted metal. Our team had been tasked to build a new clinic next to the rubble. We erected medical tents with permanent foundations, equipped them with chairs and tables, and built an outside waiting room. We got our electricity from solar panels donated by Tesla.

Soon we had a Wi-Fi connection up and running. People showed up from all over the island, desperate to contact loved ones. Word spread, and the new High Rock clinic quickly became a community center. I sutured wounds, handed out blood pressure medication, and gave diabetics insulin. On Sunday, High Rock also served as a church. There are no hymns in the world sung with more force than those sung after a hurricane. They match the intensity of the storm itself, then rise higher.

In addition to building the High Rock site, I was part of a mobile strike team that delivered health care door-to-door to people trapped in remote communities. We asked if people needed water, antibiotics, Tylenol, or sutures. I assessed and treated forehead lacerations from debris and administered tetanus shots.

When I knocked on the door of a tiny cottage that had sustained heavy water damage, an older woman opened the door. Her big sun hat draped over her head, making her look like a deaconess in a Baptist church. She wore a blue aquamarine shirt, one of our national colors, and a matching skirt. She showed me a wound on the lateral side of her forearm that had recently been sutured, but the stitches were coming loose on one end.

"Let me tend to that," I told her, cradling her arm in my hand.

I cleaned the wound with water, gauzed it up, made sure it was sterile, and restitched it. The woman thanked me, exhaustion weighing down her voice, then went back to cleaning her home. Her bravery while she lived alone in this storm made me want to build lasting change on the island.

Driving back to the clinic, I saw two young boys throwing a football around. Of course, I couldn't resist. I got out of the car and ran a few drills with them. As they sweated and panted in exertion, they beamed in happiness. It was a feeling I knew so well. Sports can make outside worries disappear, if only for a few moments. But those moments are powerful enough to keep you striving.

When I stopped into Solomon's, our local grocery store, to buy water, people would say, "I'm proud of you," and just keep walking. They were thankful, but they had an island to rebuild. We all had work to do.

During my final days on the island, I represented the International Medical Corps at the joint NGO sessions. We conferenced about the services we had provided and how we could collaborate to serve the population better. I made my voice heard, talking about the success we'd had with the internet at the clinic. I said that lasting infrastructure had to be a component of any global health program.

A member of Parliament was at one of the NGO meetings. I

invited him to come to the High Road clinic. He attended Sunday service and listened to the people's needs. Afterward, the entire congregation walked with our medical team from the clinic to the sea. We sang as we moved toward the shore. "He holds the winds in his hand, and he is the great I am . . . What a mighty God we serve," we boomed as one, singing our sorrows into the ocean.

After two weeks of nonstop work, I felt encouraged that our team had made a difference and also uplifted by the spirit of the Bahamian people. Pompey's spirit was alive and well. No storm could wash that away.

Before I headed back to the comforts of home, I took stock of what this disaster had taught me. The only thing that limited us was a lack of money and resources. NGOs and governments needed to believe in my vision for global health. To do that, I resolved to become 2 percent better at telling the story of the people I wanted to advocate for. Donors want to see faces, not facts. I also needed to become 2 percent better at forming local partnerships, working with people who had social and cultural capital on the ground.

Most importantly, I needed to get 2 percent better at listening to the needs of those I professed to serve. If I wasn't aligned with the spirit of the community, I'd be serving only myself.

● ● ●

A few months after I returned from the Bahamas, Latoya and I tied the knot in Orlando. A few weeks later, we had another ceremony in the Bahamas for my family who couldn't afford to come to the States.

As the sun set over the Atlantic Ocean, I whisked Latoya out to the dance floor. I signaled the DJ, and Stevie Wonder's "For Once in My Life" boomed from the sound system. Latoya put her head on my chest, singing the lyrics into my beating heart. *"For once I can touch what my heart used to dream of . . . For once in my life, I won't let sorrow hurt me."*

As I swayed with my wife in my arms, I knew that, for once in my life, I'd found someone who loved me, who understood me, and would be with me until I took my last breath.

For once in my life, I'd been able to stand up to racism. I hadn't let my emotions prevent me from becoming a better surgeon. For once in my life, I'd been able to serve the islands that I called home. I had stepped into my role as a doctor who served the world.

For once in my life, I felt like the man my parents had dreamed I'd become.

For once in my life my vision matched my reality.

Chapter 10

YOUR LIFE IS NOT YOUR OWN (CONTINUED)

A few days before the end of 2019, Latoya came to Boston to celebrate New Year's. She still had to finish her dental residency in Birmingham, forcing us, for the moment, to live apart. The moment she walked through the door, her presence made the utilitarian apartment feel like a home. One night, as she got ready for a hospital holiday party, I listened from another room as her voice bounced along with Stevie Wonder's silky falsetto.

"Isn't she lovely," I crooned when she emerged, looking radiant in a black dress.

"Not so bad yourself. Grab your sports coat," she said. "I hung it for you."

In our bedroom, something on the bed caught my eye. A blue onesie had been placed on top of the pillows. Below it sat two tiny booties, one pink, one blue. I picked up the onesie and read the lettering on the front: *Daddy of two.*

I felt someone behind me and turned around. Latoya stood in the doorway, clutching a baggie full of pregnancy tests.

I took a baby sock in each hand and moved toward my wife. "Twins?"

"Twins," she said, running a finger down the fabric of the baby socks.

I took Latoya into my arms and kissed her forehead.

"How many tests did you take?" I asked.

"Five," she said. "I had to make sure."

"It must have happened on our honeymoon."

"In the Bahamas," she said. "The dates line up."

"You know, I'll be the seventh neurosurgeon in our department to have twins," I said. "There must be something in the water at Mass General."

Latoya and I floated through the last week of the year, exultant and expectant. Boston finally had a bout of good weather, and our hopes for 2020 seemed as bright as the booming, dark blue sky. We attended service at Morning Star Baptist Church. Bishop Borders stood at the pulpit in a gray suit, arms stretched out, and read a prayer Jeremiah offered to God: "LORD, I know that people's lives are not their own; it is not for them to direct their steps" (Jeremiah 10:23).

The verse jogged a memory from childhood—Daddy's deep voice, speaking across the kitchen table: "Myron, your life is not your own." As a boy, I had taken the words to mean that my parents had sacrificed to make sure my brothers and I had every opportunity. My repayment for this sacrifice was to honor my parents by excelling in all I did. By following this principle for decades, I built a strong version of myself that couldn't be torn apart by adversity or exterior influence.

Now, as I worshiped beside my pregnant wife, my father's words acquired another layer of meaning. My life belonged to my unborn children. When I pictured serving them each coming day, I didn't feel the weight of sacrifice. I felt the joy of offering an oblation to God. When their time came, my children would continue our family's legacy, passing their own gifts through the generations.

• • •

The day Latoya left Boston, the weather turned. A hard, slanting rain battered the car as we drove to the airport. At the terminal, I kissed her goodbye, placing my hand on her stomach.

"I'll see you in Alabama soon," I told her. "I can't wait to get back to that Southern sunshine."

"The three of us will miss you," she said.

"Keep that precious cargo safe."

I watched Latoya's figure disappear into the throng of a security line. As I waited for a break in the rain, I caught a snippet of CNN on the wall of airport television screens. "The novel coronavirus that has emerged in China is rapidly spreading. The city of Wuhan, and its eleven million residents, are under strict quarantine," the anchor intoned. "How could eleven million people be effectively quarantined?" I wondered. On a hospital floor, a patient's simple cold could infect half the staff within a few hours.

A few weeks later, an email appeared in my inbox: *In response to the global health crisis brought on by COVID-19, Mass General has enacted institution-wide protocols that prohibit travel to conferences, meetings, and rotations.* "This seems like an extreme move," I thought. Then in early February, Harvard Medical School shut down in-person classes. The hospital's virologists and epidemiologists warned our staff that this was only the beginning. The first week of March, Latoya FaceTimed me with more bad news.

"They just shut down my dentistry program," she said. Through the phone screen, I could see worry etched across her face.

"Getting into the hospital feels like going through airport security."

"I'm scared, Myron."

"This virus isn't going to be some passing thing. We need to start thinking long term."

"I'm going to come up to Boston. You need me there. I'll stay with you until this is over."

"I want you here, but it's not safe," I said. "I may be exposed to this virus at work. I could get you and the babies sick. I won't take that chance."

"Myron, what are we going to do?"

"Go to Georgia. Go to your family. Stock up and stay put."

"I . . . I don't know when I'm going to see you again," Latoya said, her voice on the edge of breaking.

"I'm there with you all the time," I said. "You're carrying a piece of me inside you."

"FaceTime me every day."

"You know I will."

"I love you."

Before we hung up, Latoya and I reached out our fingers to meet through the screen. The truncated, digital touch wasn't enough, but it was 2 percent better than no touch at all.

When Latoya's face disappeared, a knot formed in my chest. I hadn't met my children yet, and already an invisible virus had separated me from my family. I wanted to rub Latoya's back when she had morning sickness. I wanted to feel the twins kick against her stomach. I went to the window, looking out at the cars passing on the Zakim Bridge. The world looked the same, yet I knew it had changed in some fundamental way. Blinding white light glinted off the Charles River, and I turned my eyes away from the glare.

I paced around the apartment, feeling all the plans I had spent years crafting evaporating in the face of this new threat. That August, I was supposed to go to Kenya to operate on children with hydrocephalus. I wouldn't be getting on a plane to Africa anytime soon.

I forced myself to interrupt my racing thoughts. If I sat and stewed on how circumstances had thwarted my plans, I would only

feel more helpless. Right now all I could do was focus on the present. "Small steps," I told myself. I slowed my breathing, frustration
and resentment leaving my body—2 percent more in control of my
emotions. "Boston needs doctors. You can be productive here"—2
percent clearer on my mission. "You must find a way to help your
hospital through this crisis"—2 percent more purpose-driven. That
night was difficult, but by shifting my mindset to the 2% Way, I
inched toward some semblance of control in a world that was spi-
raling toward disaster.

● ● ●

A long line snaked out from the blue awning over the entrance to
Mass General. Doctors and nurses stood shivering in their scrubs,
N95 face masks obscuring their faces. I took my place in the queue,
shielding my eyes against the late winter light bouncing off the hospital's glass facade. An ambulance screamed up to the emergency
department. A pair of EMTs hustled an elderly woman with an
oxygen mask over her face into the ED.

I moved through the line, readying my digital COVID badge.
No shortness of breath. No fever. No exposure events. I flashed the
green icon on my phone to the security guard, had my temperature
checked, and stepped into the lobby.

The hospital was unnaturally quiet. The cafeteria stood empty,
its chairs stacked against the wall. The silence magnified the sound
of my footsteps as I walked toward the elevator.

I got off on the third floor, entering the neurosurgery unit. Here
too an unwelcome eeriness clung to the usually bustling halls. A
week ago our department had ten rooms full of patients. Now, in
early March, all elective surgeries had been halted. All but one of
our rooms had been converted into COVID units. Our pressur-
ized facilities could handle the enhanced isolation and respiratory
precautions our new patients would require. For now these rooms

sat as empty as the shelves in our OR—we had given our personal protective equipment (PPE) to the emergency department.

The *click-clack* of a gurney's wheels broke the silence. Orderlies wheeled a line of children toward the elevator. We were relocating our pediatric patients to Boston Children's Hospital: we needed their beds to make room for the surge.

The surge. Harvard's virologists warned that the virus would hit Boston hard with so many people traveling through the northeast corridor. Through the windows, I saw two large trucks pull up to a shipping bay. I called Latoya as I watched men unload respirators and boxes of PPE.

"How are you holding up, Momma?" I asked.

"I'm as okay as anyone else, I suppose," she said. "My blood pressure is a bit high."

"We need to keep an eye on that. It can develop into preeclampsia."

"Dr. Williams is on top of it," Latoya said, referencing our ob-gyn. "How's it going on the front lines?"

"Mass General looks like it's preparing for a siege. We don't have many COVID patients yet, but they're coming. It feels like the day before a hurricane hits in the Bahamas."

"Don't be in COVID rooms more than you have to," she said.

"I'll try," I said. I didn't want to tell her that soon every room in the hospital would be a COVID room.

"The twins need a daddy as much as those patients need a doctor."

"No virus is going to stop that."

"I know, Myron."

"I'm getting paged," I said. "I love you. I'll call you when I get home."

The page came from Dr. Bob Carter, the chair of our department of neurosurgery. All of Mass General's neurosurgeons gathered on a Zoom call. We were all in attendance, including Dr. Curry and Dr. Brian Nahed, an attending I often operated alongside. It felt as if we were brothers in arms waiting to receive orders from a general and that those orders would bring us in the line of enemy fire.

"I don't have to tell you what's been happening around here," Dr. Carter said. "By April we expect ICUs at Mass General to be overcapacity. We've set up a surge clinic to relieve strain on the emergency department. We need bodies. You'll evaluate patients and administer COVID tests. I'm not going to say it's not dangerous, because it is. Any takers?"

I hesitated. I had just told Latoya I wouldn't expose myself to the virus without reason. But I couldn't stand idle when the need was so great. Pompey had had a family; that didn't prevent him from heading into nearly certain death.

As Dr. Carter scanned the group, a verse from Isaiah that Latoya and I had studied over the phone a few nights prior sprang to mind: "I heard the voice of the Lord saying, 'Whom shall I send? And who will go for us?' And I said, 'Here am I. Send me!'" (Isaiah 6:8).

My hand shot up. "I'll volunteer, sir."

"Good man, Dr. Rolle," Dr. Carter said.

More hands raised. My colleagues didn't hesitate to risk their lives to help strangers. Pride rang through my heart as I watched my department step up to the plate.

"No time like the present," Dr. Carter said. "Volunteers, go on down to the ED. You've got your marching orders."

I headed down to the indoor ambulance bay where the surge clinic had been erected. It was a miniature hospital within a hospital: four clinical spaces separated by temporary plastic walls served as exam rooms. Waiting room chairs had been placed six feet apart and were cleaned constantly by environmental services staff. It reminded me of the High Rock clinic I had helped build after Hurricane Dorian.

Down here, nurse practitioners ran the show. They explained how to intake patients from the street. "You perform the history and physical," one of them told us. "We document the encounter and order any laboratory tests you recommend."

I wasn't a pulmonologist or an epidemiologist—I had to learn on the fly. Just like in football, if I'm called to do something I wasn't expecting, I adjust. Luckily, doctors from all over Mass General had assembled at the surge clinic, ready to share their knowledge. Whether they delivered babies, removed brain tumors, or cut off skin tags, everyone pitched in.

I learned how to order a CT chest scan—2 percent better at diagnosing. I studied the system that helped me coordinate with the proper labs—2 percent faster at moving patients through the proper channels. I learned to notice when a lab value indicated a red flag—2 percent more perceptive. I talked to a pulmonologist I could call when a patient's symptoms stumped me—add 2 percent to my communication skills and 2 percent to my willingness to reach out for help.

I continued my education when I returned home from the hospital. This novel disease was like a personnel package in football that we'd never seen before. I had to study it to combat it, as I had studied Tim Tebow's throwing patterns when we played Florida. I read articles in the *New England Journal of Medicine* and the *American Journal of Medicine* about what combination of PPE was most effective—2 percent safer on the front lines. I combed through early COVID studies from China and Italy. They had been hit harder earlier and had initial figures on comorbidities and risk factors. When I talked to patients, I could reassure them through statistics or give them examples of patients who fit their profile—2 percent better at providing compassionate, informed care. I watched Mass General's virtual library videos about recognizing dangerous oxygen saturation rates and oscillation techniques during spontaneous ventilation—2 percent more equipped to handle an emergency.

When I hit the wall, I FaceTimed Latoya. She answered from the room that would become the twins' nursery. She swung the camera around, showing me the matching cribs.

"I come in here when I miss you," she said. "So this is where I spend most of my time at night."

"Baby," I said, "I made a choice today."

"Am I going to like what you're about to tell me?"

"I volunteered for the COVID surge clinic," I said. "They need bodies. Some days I'm going to be working twenty-four-hour shifts. I know you said . . . we talked about . . . Latoya, I couldn't just stand by. People are dying."

Latoya paused for a moment. I watched my screen as she went to a dresser and removed a Bible. "For he has not despised or scorned the suffering of the afflicted one; he has not hidden his face from him but has listened to his cry for help," she read. "Psalm 22:24. Myron, you made the right choice. I trust you."

In that moment I fell 2 percent more in love with the woman who understood the sacrifice of living a life that is not your own.

● ● ●

At 5:00 a.m. I woke in darkness. An ambulance wailed by in the street below. As soon as the sound faded, another replaced it. Now, in the late days of March, their sirens had become ubiquitous. I rose, shaking the soreness from my muscles.

I opened my laptop in my kitchen, squinted until my eyes adjusted to the screen, and read my patients' electronic medical records. Seventy percent of them had COVID-19. I showered, put on my scrubs and a black coat over my gray Mass General fleece, masked up, and left for the hospital. I would be at Mass General for the next twenty-four hours.

It was still freezing even though spring had arrived. The frigid weather was more than a nuisance—it created a perfect condition for the spread of the virus. I listened to soca music, which put a bop in my step as I made my way alone through dark downtown Boston. The city had been in quarantine for weeks—my only companions on the street were a few Uber drivers idling through downtown.

By five thirty, I had made it through the security line. After dousing my hands in sanitizer, I pulled a fresh N95 mask tight over my ears and donned goggles. Then I made my rounds. I stayed in each room no longer than five minutes. Time was one of our greatest resources. I had to distribute it as fairly and efficiently as possible.

After rounds I went to a computer in a little alcove and input orders for my COVID patients. One of my patients, an older man who had come from a rehab facility, had increased respiratory compromise. His symptoms were outside my expertise, so I called one of the pulmonologists I knew. "He's over fifty, and his O2 saturations are going down," I said. "What should I do?"

"Increase his vent settings," the pulmonologist replied. "And let's make sure that we're getting serial scans to track the progress of the bilateral pulmonary infiltrates."

"Roger that," I said.

"Working a twenty-four?"

"You know it."

"I don't know how you get through it without coffee. Good luck."

At one o'clock my pager beeped—the emergency department needed assistance. I relied on respiratory doctors to help me with my COVID patients; they relied on me to help ED patients with neurosurgical issues. Sharing our expertise allowed us to improve patient care by 2 percent.

In the bowels of the ED, doctors and nurses scrambled by, shouting in desperation over the din for assistance and supplies. The nurses were pushed to their limit—many of them weren't used to tending to such acutely ill patients. I turned a corner and saw a woman being intubated.

"Let's get respiratory here, stat. I need succinylcholine. I need paralytics. I need IVs placed," an ED doctor yelled.

The respirator emitted quickening beeps as the patient's oxygen saturation crept downward. Staff ran into the room. They lifted his head, moved his tongue out of the way, and inserted the tube to give the patient succinylcholine. He stabilized, kept alive for now.

"What happened?" I asked one of the nurses in the hallway.

"Twenty minutes ago, he was talking to his family, and then boom," she said. "Next thing you know, he was desatting, and we needed to intubate him."

"He went downhill so quickly."

"Sometimes it happens faster than that. Those are the ones we can't save," she said. "I've seen more death and suffering in the last month than in my whole career."

"We'll make it through this," I said.

"We had better," the nurse replied and hustled off.

I made my way to my patient's room. I donned a new set of PPE before I entered. He'd come to the ED complaining of shortness of breath, naturally worried that he had COVID. His COVID results hadn't returned yet, but a CT scan had revealed a lesion in his parietal lobe.

When I entered the room, the man sat up on his elbows, eyes wide with fear. "Did my COVID results come back?" he asked before I could introduce myself.

"I'm Dr. Rolle," I replied. "I'm a neurosurgery resident here at Mass General. Your COVID results haven't come back yet. But they should soon."

"I was exposed," he said. "Twice."

"Your oxygen levels are stable," I said, trying to reassure him. "We need to talk about your brain tumor."

"Can I take another test?" he asked. "If I have the virus, I won't be able to work. I can't lose my job."

"Let's wait for the results," I said.

"What about hydroxychloroquine?" he asked. "I heard on Fox News that might work."

"We don't even know if you have COVID. We need to talk about next steps for treatment for your tumor."

Finally, the patient calmed down and let me walk him through his options, agreeing to have surgery. This man had a brain tumor, but he was more concerned about his COVID status. His mindset seemed irrational, but I could understand it. People were dying all around him. The news constantly beamed in reports of disaster. His mental state illustrated the degree to which this virus had infiltrated our psyches.

I left the patient's room and walked past the surge clinic. The line stretched beyond my field of vision. I saw providers intaking patients and determining who needed a test. Everyone wanted one, of course, but they were in short supply. Testing required so much of our time and resources that they had to be reserved for those who needed them most. I'm sure providers hated having to say no to people with fear in their eyes, but all we could do was educate them about self-isolation and give them a discharge packet with a mask.

During a short break, I ducked into a quiet hallway and called Latoya.

"Did you eat today?" she asked me.

"I may have missed a meal. Or two."

"You have to take care of yourself," she said.

"Let me say hi to the twins, please," I said. "That takes care of me."

I heard a rustle as Latoya put the phone to her stomach. I closed my eyes, picturing them growing healthy and strong. "Daddy will see you soon," I said.

After I said goodbye, I devoured a sandwich standing up and returned to my post. Hours later I walked home before the morning sun rose. The streets were empty, and though delirious, I cherished the moment of solitude. In my apartment, I hit the bed with a thud like I had been dropped from a high altitude. Dreamless sleep overtook my exhausted body.

What seemed like minutes later, the jingle of my phone woke me. "Hello?" I answered, my voice still thick with sleep.

"Dr. Rolle? Wright Thompson."

Thompson, an ESPN journalist, had written a story about me

while I was at Oxford in 2010. He was one of the few writers who understood that my NFL dreams and academic career were not at odds with each other.

"It's nice to hear a voice from the sports world," I said.

"You sound beat."

"I am. I just got off a twenty-four-hour shift. The hospital is overrun with COVID patients."

"I thought you were a neurosurgeon."

"I am, but it's all hands on deck."

"Myron, stories are my job. And this is a story."

Thompson asked if I could film my next marathon shift with my phone. From my footage, he crafted a segment that aired on ESPN's *Outside the Lines*. The piece went viral, racking up five million views on Instagram and ninety thousand likes on my personal Facebook page. Within hours, reporters from *Good Morning America*, the *Washington Post*, CNN, and a bevy of sports talk shows jammed my inbox with interview requests. I saw the publicity as a way to spread a vital message. As I prepped for the interviews, I framed my talking points in language that would stimulate sports fans. I wanted to use my platform as an athlete to inform people about 2 percent of the on-the-ground reality of this pandemic. If people gleaned even a small amount of knowledge from my words, I felt like I would be doing my part as a citizen in a global health crisis.

I also wanted to sound the alarm about the racial disparities in health care. These existed before the pandemic and, with the onset of COVID-19, were causing disproportionate suffering and death in minority communities. In densely populated urban centers, social distancing was impossible. And for many, staying at home was not an option. Where would the food come from? How would bills be paid? If a Black or Brown person was an essential worker in a community with public transportation, they were at a higher risk of contracting the virus and spreading it within crowded multigenerational living conditions.

For the next two months, I appeared on dozens of shows. Charles Barkley and Ernie Johnson interviewed me on *Inside the NBA*. Keyshawn Johnson and Jay Williams let me talk about why I thought the NFL should cancel the rest of the season, a take I caught some flack for from listeners. Pat McAfee let me spread my message to his millions of podcast listeners and kidded me about running for president.

There are lessons to learn from those dark days of the pandemic. It taught the American medical system that we need to get 2 percent better at extending ourselves to marginalized communities. We must go to them rather than waiting for a crisis to force action. It taught us that we need to improve 2 percent in our pandemic preparedness. If we are ready for a public health crisis, we can respond to it while still caring for patients with other health issues. People don't stop having cancer and diabetes in a pandemic. It taught me that I needed to get 2 percent better at educating people, especially Black and Brown people, about managing chronic conditions.

$$\bullet \ \bullet \ \bullet$$

On the first warm day in April, I was putting in a shift as the consult resident when my pager rang. Dr. Nahed, my attending, needed me for emergency surgery. I made my way to the third floor, excited to get back in the OR.

"This one is going to be a challenge," Dr. Nahed said when I met him. "COVID-19, HIV-positive, and suffering from cryptococcal meningitis."

"I'm ready to go," I told him.

"I know you are, that's why I want you to take the lead."

Cryptococcal meningitis is a debilitating and potentially fatal fungal infection of the brain. It had created cysts that were blocking the patient's ventricles, causing high intracranial pressure. I looked over the patient's chart, my eyes scanning the long list of comorbidities. Surgery was extremely risky for a man in his condition. But if we didn't operate, he would die.

"We need to insert a . . ."

"Ventriculoperitoneal shunt," I said.

"That's right. Do you have experience with this procedure?"

"I do," I said, frowning.

Ventriculoperitoneal shunt. The words stirred a prick of anxiety. This was the procedure that had long caused me trouble. By applying the 2% Way, I'd performed the surgery successfully on an infant, but that had been more than a year ago. I hadn't had the opportunity to try it again. Would my old mistakes resurface? The high-risk nature of the patient compounded my fears. We would have to move with pinpoint precision; there could be no extra blood flow anywhere, given his HIV-positive status. With such a fragile body, ravaged by COVID and years of smoking, speed was vital. There was no time for mistakes. My technique had to be flawless, a far cry from how nervous and ineffective my movements had been as a green resident.

While the anesthesiologist intubated the patient, the surgical team stepped outside the OR—a new precaution. After the anesthesiologist inserted the tube down the patient's trachea, she covered his head with a plastic vent-like apparatus that would keep respiratory particles from spreading. We needed to wait twenty minutes for the ventilation system to clean the air.

I used this time to think back to my successful operation on the infant. I retraced my motions, remembering exactly where I had made my incisions. My surgical plan became 2 percent more precise. I remembered the feeling I had when I told the infant's mother that her baby was going to be okay. My confidence grew. I was ready. Dr. Nahed and I strapped on our PPE and headed into the OR.

Nervous energy filled the room. I took up my scalpel, working my way through the subcutaneous tissue and down through the galea. When I reached the bone, I adeptly employed a perforator to open a hole that revealed the dura.

Now I had to deal with the abdomen. The patient was very thin, so every cut into his abdomen had to be exact. I paused, taking as deep a breath as my N95 mask would allow, then proceeded. I utilized my tools with gentle but exact movements, making my way through his abdominal muscles, past his peritoneal wall, and into his bowel. I was fluid, my cuts were perfect.

I moved back to the head and opened the dura. After a series of small incisions in the neck, it was time to tunnel from the head to the abdomen. I sent the tunneler down, passing it under the skin. It held in place, stopping at its intended resting place in the stomach. I passed the distal catheter within the tunneler, then inserted the proximal catheter into the frontal aspect of the ventricles. Fluid drained from the patient's brain. The entire catheter system was then connected, the distal catheter was dunked into the peritoneal space and the incisions were all closed.

"He's stable," Dr. Nahed said. "Strong work, Dr. Rolle."

• • •

The next few months were a blur, as the first surge of the pandemic taxed the hospital to the breaking point. There was more than enough pain and trauma for a lifetime. But little by little, things improved, and by summer the situation had stabilized to the point where we could breathe a slight sigh of relief under our masks.

I had personal reasons to be hopeful for the future. In August 2020, Latoya gave birth to a healthy baby girl and boy. When I held my children for the first time, a joy I had never known filled my heart. As I learned how to change diapers and burp a baby, I thought about the future I wanted my children to inherit. When our twins returned to their ancestral home in the Caribbean, I wanted the surgical health system to be strong enough to care for them and others in their generation.

Most people see the Caribbean as a tropical paradise of sunshine, clear seas, and sweet cocktails. But behind the idyllic veil created by the tourism industry are fifteen nations with swaths of citizens who don't have access to adequate medical care. When it comes to head trauma and brain-related medical issues, the dearth of care is even worse. There are only forty-two neurosurgeons to serve the sixteen million people in the CARICOM region, and the majority of these neurosurgeons and their facilities are understaffed and under-funded. The number of preventable deaths is heartbreaking. I know because my Auntie Annie was one of these unnecessary victims.

Annie Gwendolyn Rolle Smith was technically my cousin on my father's side. Whenever I went back to Exuma, I'd accompany my family on a visit to Auntie Annie to "hail" her, a Bahamian term for paying respects. She lived on Exuma in a yellow one-story bungalow from which she ruled as the matriarch over that side of our family. The house was constantly bathed in gold light that poured in from her wide-open windows. I can still smell the peas 'n' rice that were always simmering on her sky-blue stove and the sweet aroma of her flowers and plants that decorated every corner of the house. We'd sit in the cool shade on her porch and drink Goombay Punch while she dispensed wisdom.

When older Bahamians talk, their words are usually infused with reverence to God. "Hey, Auntie, how's life treating you?" I asked her during a visit in 2009, just before I was to enter the NFL draft.

"Oh, child, I'm right here breathing. God's good," she replied as she bustled around, making everyone plates of food. I hadn't men-tioned God, but she found a way to work him into the conversation.

Shortly after that trip, I was drafted by the Titans. While I sat in the locker room of the Titans training facility after practice, Daddy called me. Auntie Annie, he said, had died. We'd seen her only a couple of months before, and that made the loss especially painful. Then he told me what happened.

Annie was walking early in the morning to her local market

when a car careened around the street corner. It hit her, and the driver took off. She laid on the ground alone for over an hour until a passerby found her and rushed her to the local clinic in Georgetown, a settlement in Exuma.

There was no nurse or physician at the clinic. Auntie Annie didn't receive an MRI or CT scan. My Exuma family tried desperately to get in touch with physicians in Nassau to initiate a medical evacuation. But the lines of communication were dead. In this situation, "winter residents" from Europe or America could afford to call a medical evacuation team to carry the patient from Exuma to Florida in thirty minutes. Bahamians who don't have that kind of money are at the mercy of a challenged government health care system.

As she waited in the clinic, uncared for, Auntie Annie became sleepy. Her body weakened. After a short time, she slipped into a coma and died seven hours later. She never saw a single doctor.

I'm certain Annie had a brain bleed. The human skull is a fixed box that can contain only a certain volume. Expanding blood in Annie's skull caused her brain to move and shift. The more the brain stem shifts, the higher the likelihood you'll slip into a coma.

Just as much as from the accident, Auntie Annie's death resulted from a broader, more systemic problem in the Caribbean. The region's geography exacerbates the issue of health care delivery. Long distances between islands and a lack of a central medical hub make getting treatment for head trauma within the recommended four-hour window almost impossible. And so preventable death happens across the Caribbean, especially in communities on remote islands.

It pained me to know that if my auntie had been struck by a car in Boston, a simple procedure requiring a few burr holes would have saved her life. She would have left the hospital in two days, and I would have danced with her at my wedding in the Bahamas. Back in 2010, I knew I had to do something to stop this type of tragedy. But I didn't yet have the tools or the resources.

Since that time, I've taken countless small steps to become the kind of leader who can enact that level of structural change. From President Clinton, I learned how to get 2 percent better at fundraising. My time in the NFL made me 2 percent better at handling setbacks. And Latoya gave me a model for true selflessness.

Now I am spearheading something called the Caribbean Neurosurgery Foundation. This initiative seeks to utilize the political unity that exists among Caribbean nations—instead of operating in silos, Caribbean doctors will exchange patient data and best practices. I've been petitioning the government, asking for more operating rooms, more financial investments into neurosurgical care, and more training opportunities for the Caribbean's medical workforce.

I see this initiative—and the others I plan to implement across the world—as the ultimate fulfillment of the 2% Way. Every English morning spent running sprints with Cory, every piece of wisdom and love I collected from Mummy and Daddy, every long night studying medical journals, every time I refused to choose between academics and athletics slowly created a leader.

I have football to thank. From the moment Mickey Andrews first told me about the 2% Way in a sweaty football locker room, this philosophy has steered my life. It got me through Florida State, Oxford, the NFL, Harvard, through the front lines of a global pandemic, and now back to the Bahamas where it all began, solving health issues in the country of my origin. The philosophy of growth through small incremental steps has carried me through each challenge I faced as an immigrant, academic, doctor, athlete, husband, father, and nephew. Through the 2% Way, I moved beyond the quick anger of my boyhood. I fulfilled the promise of my parents' sacrifice. I earned the respect and friendship of my teammates on and off the field. I found the love of a woman who will be by my side until one of us takes our last breath. I stepped fully into an identity that many refused to admit existed.

The 2% Way helped me build a life full of purpose and meaning. It can do the same for you. It takes away the pressure you feel when your problems seem insurmountable. If you see your life from a thirty-thousand-foot view, your challenges will seem as large as the earth. But if you take tangible, incremental steps of edification every day, that which was once overwhelming will shrink to a manageable size. Progress becomes reality.

Whether you are trying to grow closer to God, trying to yoke yourself to the right partner, trying to create a family or provide for one, trying to become a leader for people on the margins, or trying to find your identity, the 2% Way will give you the tools to tackle life with the assuredness that you are taking steps in the right direction. When you look back on all those steps, you will realize that each one was valuable, that each one changed you.

And in the process of changing yourself, you will find that you have changed the world.

NOTES

Prologue: Pressure Points

1. Audre Lorde, *Sister Outsider: Essays and Speeches by Audre Lorde* (Berkeley: Crossing, 2007), 146.

Chapter 1: Your Life Is Not Your Own

1. Ben Carson with Cecil B. Murphey, *Gifted Hands: The Ben Carson Story* (Grand Rapids: Zondervan, 1990), 98.

Chapter 4: The Colossus of Rhodes

1. Cecil John Rhodes, *The Last Will and Testament of Cecil John Rhodes: With Elucidatory Notes to Which Are Added Some Chapters Describing the Political and Religious Ideas of the Testator*, ed. W. T. Stead (London: Review of Reviews Office, 1902), 36.
2. Wright Thompson, "The Burden of Being Myron Rolle," *ESPN: Outside the Lines*, 2010, accessed December 14, 2021, http://www .espn.com/espn/eticket/story?page=100218/myronrolle.
3. Thompson, "The Burden of Being Myron Rolle."

Chapter 5: 32 / 32

1. Aldous Huxley, "Variations on a Philosopher," in *Themes and Variations* (London: Chatto & Windus, 1915), 66.
2. Lee Hawkins, "Can Scholars Make Dollars in the NFL?," *Wall Street Journal*, December 21, 2009, https://www.wsj.com/articles/SB100014 24052748704238104574602350196862702.

Chapter 6: With the 207th Pick . . .

1. D. Hyde, "Myron Rolle a Hit at Senior Bowl; Lay Off Tebow," *South Florida Sun Sentinel*, January 28, 2010.
2. Associated Press, "Rolle Goes from Rhodes Scholar to Titans Safety in Sixth Round," NFL.com, April 24, 2010, https://www.nfl.com /news/rolle-goes-from-rhodes-scholar-to-titans-safety-in-sixth -round-09000d5d817c5373.
3. Jemele Hill, "Myron Rolle's Sad Draft Fall," ESPN, April 28, 2010, https://www.espn.com/nfl/story/_/id/5142229.

Chapter 8: A Rookie Again

1. This conversation is Dr. Rolle's recollection of the interview, which is discussed in Jacqueline Howard, "Myron Rolle's Journey from NFL to Neurosurgery," CNN, May 22, 2017, https://www.cnn .com/2017/05/19/health/myron-rolle-nfl-medical-school-profile /index.html.

Chapter 9: For Once in My Life

1. C. Wekon-Kemeni, "Latoya Legrand, D.D.S.," Black Man, M.D., September 27, 2018, https://blackmanmd.com/latoya-legrand-d-d-s/.